CONFRONTING GLOBAL WARMING

Farming and the Food Supply

CONFRONTING GLOBAL WARMING

Farming and the Food Supply

Debra A. Miller

Michael E. Mann
Consulting Editor

GREENHAVEN PRESS
A part of Gale, Cengage Learning

GALE
CENGAGE Learning

Detroit • New York • San Francisco • New Haven, Conn • Waterville, Maine • London

GALE
CENGAGE Learning™

Christine Nasso, *Publisher*
Elizabeth Des Chenes, *Managing Editor*

© 2011 Greenhaven Press, a part of Gale, Cengage Learning

For more information, contact:

Greenhaven Press
27500 Drake Rd.
Farmington Hills, MI 48331-3535
Or you can visit our Internet site at gale.cengage.com.

For product information and technology assistance, contact us at
Gale Customer Support, 1-800-877-4253.

For permission to use material from this text or product, submit all requests online at
www.cengage.com/permissions.

Further permissions questions can be e-mailed to permissionrequest@cengage.com

Every effort is made to ensure that Greenhaven Press accurately reflects the original intent of the authors. Every effort has been made to trace the owners of copyrighted material.

Cover image © 2011 Photos.com, a division of Getty Images. All rights reserved. Leaf image copyright © JinYoung Lee, 2010, used under license from Shutterstock.com. Leaf icon © iStockPhoto.com/domin_domin.

**LIBRARY OF CONGRESS
CATALOGING-IN-PUBLICATION DATA**
Miller, Debra A.
    Farming and the food supply / by Debra A. Miller.
        p. cm. -- (Confronting global warming)
    Includes bibliographical references and index.
    ISBN 978-0-7377-5173-4 (hardcover)
    1. Crops and climate--Environmental aspects. 2. Plants--Effect of global warming on. 3. Climatic changes--Environmental aspects. 4. Food supply--Environmental aspects. 5. Global warming. I. Title.
    S600.7.G56M55 2011
    338.1'9--dc22
                                              2010046611

Printed in the United States of America
1 2 3 4 5 6 7 15 14 13 12 11

Contents

Preface

*"The warnings about global warming
have been extremely clear for a long
time. We are facing a global climate
crisis. It is deepening. We are entering
a period of consequences."*

Al Gore

Still hotly debated by some, human-induced global warming is now accepted in the scientific community. Earth's average yearly temperature is getting steadily warmer; sea levels are rising due to melting ice caps; and the resulting impact on ocean life, wildlife, and human life is already evident. The human-induced buildup of greenhouse gases in the atmosphere poses serious and diverse threats to life on earth. As scientists work to develop accurate models to predict the future impact of global warming, researchers, policy makers, and industry leaders are coming to terms with what can be done today to halt and reverse the human contributions to global climate change.

Each volume in the Confronting Global Warming series examines the current and impending challenges the planet faces because of global warming. Several titles focus on a particular aspect of life—such as weather, farming, health, or nature and wildlife—that has been altered by climate change. Consulting the works of leading experts in the field, Confronting Global Warming authors present the current status of those aspects as they have been affected by global warming, highlight key future challenges, examine potential solutions for dealing with the results of climate change, and address the pros and cons of imminent changes and challenges. Other volumes in the series—such as those dedicated to the role of government, the role of industry, and the role of the individual—address the impact various facets of society can have on climate change. The result is a series that provides students and general-interest readers with a solid understanding of the worldwide ramifications of climate change and what can be done to help humanity adapt to changing conditions and mitigate damage.

Each volume includes:

- A descriptive **table of contents** listing subtopics, charts, graphs, maps, and sidebars included in each chapter
- Full-color **charts, graphs, and maps** to illustrate key points, concepts, and theories
- Full-color **photos** that enhance textual material
- **Sidebars** that provide explanations of technical concepts or statistical information, present case studies to illustrate the international impact of global warming, or offer excerpts from primary and secondary documents
- **Pulled quotes** containing key points and statistical figures
- A **glossary** providing users with definitions of important terms
- An annotated **bibliography** of additional books, periodicals, and Web sites for further research
- A detailed **subject index** to allow users to quickly find the information they need

The Confronting Global Warming series provides students and general-interest readers with the information they need to understand the complex issue of climate change. Titles in the series offer users a well-rounded view of global warming, presented in an engaging format. Confronting Global Warming not only provides context for how society has dealt with climate change thus far but also encapsulates debates about how it will confront issues related to climate in the future.

Foreword

Earth's climate is a complex system of interacting natural components. These components include the atmosphere, the ocean, and the continental ice sheets. Living things on earth—or, the biosphere—also constitute an important component of the climate system.

Natural Factors Cause Some of Earth's Warming and Cooling

Numerous factors influence Earth's climate system, some of them natural. For example, the slow drift of continents that takes place over millions of years, a process known as plate tectonics, influences the composition of the atmosphere through its impact on volcanic activity and surface erosion. Another significant factor involves naturally occurring gases in the atmosphere, known as greenhouse gases, which have a warming influence on Earth's surface. Scientists have known about this warming effect for nearly two centuries: These gases absorb outgoing heat energy and direct it back toward the surface. In the absence of this natural greenhouse effect, Earth would be a frozen, and most likely lifeless, planet.

Another natural factor affecting Earth's climate—this one measured on timescales of several millennia—involves cyclical variations in the geometry of Earth's orbit around the sun. These variations alter the distribution of solar radiation over the surface of Earth and are responsible for the coming and going of the ice ages every one hundred thousand years or so. In addition, small variations in the brightness of the sun drive minor changes in Earth's surface temperature over decades and centuries. Explosive volcanic activity, such as the Mount Pinatubo eruption in the Philippines in 1991, also affects Earth's climate. These eruptions inject highly reflective particles called aerosol into the upper part of the atmosphere, known as the stratosphere, where they can reside for a year or longer. These particles reflect some of the incoming sunlight back into space and cool Earth's surface for years at a time.

Human Progress Puts Pressure on Natural Climate Patterns

Since the dawn of the industrial revolution some two centuries ago, however, humans have become the principal drivers of climate change. The burning of fossil fuels—such as oil, coal, and natural gas—has led to an increase in atmospheric levels of carbon dioxide, a powerful greenhouse gas. And farming practices have led to increased atmospheric levels of methane, another potent greenhouse gas. If humanity continues such activities at the current rate through the end of this century, the concentrations of greenhouse gases in the atmosphere will be higher than they have been for tens of millions of years. It is the unprecedented rate at which we are amplifying the greenhouse effect, warming Earth's surface, and modifying our climate that causes scientists so much concern.

The Role of Scientists in Climate Observation and Projection

Scientists study Earth's climate not just from observation but also from a theoretical perspective. Modern-day climate models successfully reproduce the key features of Earth's climate, including the variations in wind patterns around the globe, the major ocean current systems such as the Gulf Stream, and the seasonal changes in temperature and rainfall associated with Earth's annual revolution around the sun. The models also reproduce some of the more complex natural oscillations of the climate system. Just as the atmosphere displays random day-to-day variability that we term "weather," the climate system produces its own random variations, on timescales of years. One important example is the phenomenon called El Niño, a periodic warming of the eastern tropical Pacific Ocean surface that influences seasonal patterns of temperature and rainfall around the globe. The ability to use models to reproduce the climate's complicated natural oscillatory behavior gives scientists increased confidence that these models are up to the task of mimicking the climate system's response to human impacts.

To that end, scientists have subjected climate models to a number of rigorous tests of their reliability. James Hansen of the NASA Goddard Institute for Space Studies performed a famous experiment back in 1988, when he subjected a climate model (one relatively primitive by modern standards) to possible future fossil fuel emissions scenarios. For the scenario that most closely matches actual emissions since then, the model's predicted course of global temperature increase shows an uncanny correspondence to the actual increase in temperature over the intervening two decades. When Mount Pinatubo erupted in the Philippines in 1991, Hansen performed another famous experiment. Before the volcanic aerosol had an opportunity to influence the climate (it takes several months to spread globally throughout the atmosphere), he took the same climate model and subjected it to the estimated atmospheric aerosol distribution. Over the next two years, actual global average surface temperatures proceeded to cool a little less than 1°C (1.8°F), just as Hansen's model predicted they would.

Given that there is good reason to trust the models, scientists can use them to answer important questions about climate change. One such question weighs the human factors against the natural factors to determine responsibility for the dramatic changes currently taking place in our climate. When driven by natural factors alone, climate models do not reproduce the observed warming of the past century. Only when these models are also driven by human factors—primarily, the increase in greenhouse gas concentrations—do they reproduce the observed warming. Of course, the models are not used just to look at the past. To make projections of future climate change, climate scientists consider various possible scenarios or pathways of future human activity.

The earth has warmed roughly 1°C since preindustrial times. In the "business as usual" scenario, where we continue the current course of burning fossil fuel through the twenty-first century, models predict an additional warming anywhere from roughly 2°C to 5°C (3.6°F to 9°F). The models also show that even if we were to stop fossil fuel burning today, we are probably committed to as much as 0.6°C additional warming because of the inertia of the climate system. This inertia ensures warming for a century to come, simply due to our greenhouse gas emissions thus far. This committed warming introduces a profound procrastination penalty for not taking immediate action. If we are to avert an additional warming of 1°C, which would bring the net warming to 2°C—often considered an appropriate threshold for defining dangerous human impact on our climate—we have to act almost immediately.

Long-Term Warming May Bring About Extreme Changes Worldwide

In the "business as usual" emissions scenario, climate change will have an array of substantial impacts on our society and the environment by the end of this century. Patterns of rainfall and drought are projected to shift in such a way that some regions currently stressed for water resources, such as the desert southwest of the United States and the Middle East, are likely to become drier. More intense rainfall events in other regions, such as Europe and the midwestern United States, could lead to increased flooding. Heat waves like the one in Europe in summer 2003, which killed more than thirty thousand people, are projected to become far more common. Atlantic hurricanes are likely to reach greater intensities, potentially doing far more damage to coastal infrastructure.

Furthermore, regions such as the Arctic are expected to warm faster than the rest of the globe. Disappearing Arctic sea ice already threatens wildlife, including polar bears and walruses. Given another 2°C warming (3.6°F), a substantial portion of the

Greenland ice sheet is likely to melt. This event, combined with other factors, could lead to more than 1 meter (about 3 feet) of sea-level rise by the end of the century. Such a rise in sea level would threaten many American East Coast and Gulf Coast cities, as well as low-lying coastal regions and islands around the world. Food production in tropical regions, already insufficient to meet the needs of some populations, will probably decrease with future warming. The incidence of infectious disease is expected to increase in higher elevations and in latitudes with warming temperatures. In short, the impacts of future climate change are likely to have a devastating impact on society and our environment in the absence of intervention.

Strategies for Confronting Climate Change

Options for dealing with the threats of climate change include both adaptation to inevitable changes and mitigation, or lessening, of those changes that we can still affect. One possible adaptation would be to adjust our agricultural practices to the changing regional patterns of temperature and rainfall. Another would be to build coastal defenses against the inundation from sea-level rise. Only mitigation, however, can prevent the most threatening changes. One means of mitigation that has been given much recent attention is geoengineering. This method involves perturbing the climate system in such a way as to partly or fully offset the warming impact of rising greenhouse gas concentrations. One geoengineering approach involves periodically shooting aerosol particles, similar to ones produced by volcanic eruptions, into the stratosphere—essentially emulating the cooling impact of a major volcanic eruption on an ongoing basis. As with nearly all geoengineering proposals, there are potential perils with this scheme, including an increased tendency for continental drought and the acceleration of stratospheric ozone depletion.

The only foolproof strategy for climate change mitigation is the decrease of greenhouse gas emissions. If we are to avert a dangerous 2°C increase relative to preindustrial times, we will probably need to bring greenhouse gas emissions to a peak within the coming years and reduce them well below current levels within the coming decades. Any strategy for such a reduction of emissions must be international and multipronged, involving greater conservation of energy resources; a shift toward alternative, carbon-free sources of energy; and a coordinated set of governmental policies that encourage responsible corporate and individual practices. Some contrarian voices argue that we cannot afford to take such steps. Actually, given the procrastination penalty of not acting on the climate change problem, what we truly cannot afford is to delay action.

Evidently, the problem of climate change crosses multiple disciplinary boundaries and involves the physical, biological, and social sciences. As an issue facing all of civilization, climate change demands political, economic, and ethical considerations. With the Confronting Global Warming series, Greenhaven Press addresses all of these considerations in an accessible format. In ten thorough volumes, the series covers the full range of climate change impacts (water and ice; extreme weather; population, resources, and conflict; nature and wildlife; farming and food supply; health and disease) and the various essential components of any solution to the climate change problem (energy production and alternative energy; the role of government; the role of industry; and the role of the individual). It is my hope and expectation that this series will become a useful resource for anyone who is curious about not only the nature of the problem but also about what we can do to solve it.

Michael E. Mann

Michael E. Mann is a professor in the Department of Meteorology at Penn State University and director of the Penn State Earth System

Science Center. In 2002 he was selected as one of the fifty leading visionaries in science and technology by Scientific American. *He was a lead author for the "Observed Climate Variability and Change" chapter of the Intergovernmental Panel on Climate Change (IPCC) Third Scientific Assessment Report, and in 2007 he shared the Nobel Peace Prize with other IPCC authors. He is the author of more than 120 peer-reviewed publications, and he recently coauthored the book* Dire Predictions: Understanding Global Warming *with colleague Lee Kump. Mann is also a co-founder and avid contributor to the award-winning science Web site RealClimate.org.*

CHAPTER 1

Farming and Global Warming: An Introduction

According to the Food and Agriculture Organization of the United Nations, global warming (also called climate change) is one of the most serious threats to future food production. Rising temperatures and other weather changes, climate experts say, will negatively affect crop yields around the world. This threat comes at a critical time when agriculture is also facing predictions of exponential population growth as well as the need to decrease its own greenhouse gas emissions—gases such as carbon dioxide, nitrous oxide, and methane that are believed to be a major cause of climate change. As the world grows both warmer and more crowded, therefore, farmers will be asked to produce more and more food under increasingly challenging conditions.

A "Perfect Storm" of Challenges Ahead for Farmers

Over the past century, farmers produced enough food to feed much of the world even as the human population swelled dramatically. According to the United Nations Population Fund, global population grew from 1.6 billion to 6.1 billion people during the course of the twentieth century—a spike of 4.5 billion in little more than one hundred years. Because of significant advances in farming technology, agriculture was able to keep pace with this rapid population growth. That accomplishment became

The Effect of Population Growth on Global Warming

The rapid growth of the human population during the twentieth century, according to some commentators, is the main driver of climate change because an increased number of people inevitably raises the demand for fossil fuels and adds to the carbon dioxide and other greenhouse gases that are released into the earth's atmosphere. In fact, during the last century, when the human population grew by 4.5 billion people, carbon emissions grew twelvefold. If the world population continues to grow as predicted during the twenty-first century, carbon levels could spiral out of control, and many experts worry that the earth's environment may be altered in ways that might make the planet unable to sustain a large human population.

This close link between population and global warming has led to calls for slowing population growth. Environmental groups such as the Worldwatch Institute, for example, have argued that if the world cannot stabilize both the climate and population numbers, the earth's ecosystems simply will not survive. Yet attempts to restrict people's rights to have children have always been fraught with controversy because reproduction is viewed by many people as a basic human right. Notably, the highest birth rates typically occur in developing nations, while populations in most developed nations are stabilized or shrinking. This circumstance has led many population experts to suggest that the key to population control is education and poverty reduction—benefits that result from strong economic development. Specifically, by giving poor women and girls opportunities for health care, education, and economic advancement, advocates believe women will voluntarily choose to limit the size of their families. If this theory is correct, the most important step humans could take to limit world population growth is to promote equitable economic development in the poorest regions of the world. This development must be done in a sustainable way, however; if done using fossil fuels, such development would also increase the greenhouse gas emissions that cause global warming.

known as the Green Revolution. It was made possible largely by fossil fuels—petroleum energy that was used to power farm equipment and petrochemicals that were developed into cheap fertilizers and pesticides. An even larger population boom is now unfolding: By the middle of the twenty-first century, experts say, the worldwide population could exceed 9 billion people, and if it stays on the same trajectory, by 2085 the global population could grow to more than 12 billion. Like the last population spike, this massive increase in population will substantially raise the demand for food, freshwater, and energy. Agriculture therefore needs to achieve a second revolution in food production to keep up with this continuing population explosion.

The pressure to produce more food, however, comes at a time when farmers are also facing climate changes caused by global warming—changes that could drastically alter, and in many cases reduce, agricultural output and undermine food production. Adding to the sense of urgency, farmers during coming decades will be asked to reduce their reliance on fossil fuels and change other established farm practices because modern industrialized agriculture produces greenhouse gases and is a significant contributor to global warming. Britain's chief scientist, John Beddington, calls these challenges a "perfect storm"[1] that will complicate farming in sometimes unpredictable ways and severely test farmers' ability to feed the world population.

The Impact of Global Warming on Farming and Food Security

Unpredictable weather has always been the enemy of agriculture, but farmers have somehow managed to survive and even thrive. Throughout the twentieth century, for example, American farmers faced severe droughts, dust storms, tornadoes, floods, and wildfires. Yet between 1930 and 2000 U.S. agricultural output almost quadrupled, greatly increasing the world's supply of such crops as wheat, rice, and corn—known as cereal grains—that are critical to feeding the world. The future changes in climate

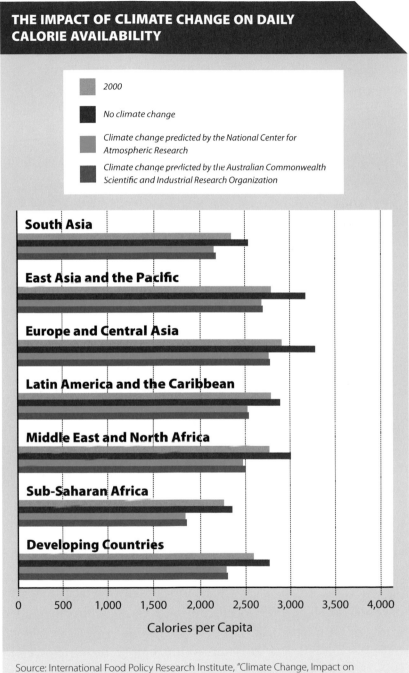

THE IMPACT OF CLIMATE CHANGE ON DAILY CALORIE AVAILABILITY

2000

No climate change

Climate change predicted by the National Center for Atmospheric Research

Climate change predicted by the Australian Commonwealth Scientific and Industrial Research Organization

South Asia

East Asia and the Pacific

Europe and Central Asia

Latin America and the Caribbean

Middle East and North Africa

Sub-Saharan Africa

Developing Countries

Calories per Capita

Source: International Food Policy Research Institute, "Climate Change, Impact on Agriculture and Costs of Adaptation," October 2009, p. 11. www.ifpri.org.

predicted by scientists, however, will make the weather even more unpredictable and will bring significant changes in climate that will negatively affect all aspects of farming, including growing seasons, water supplies, soil fertility, pests and diseases, and weed production.

The IPCC warns that average temperature increases beyond 1.8°F–3.6°F (1°C–2°C) threaten crop production of the world's major food grains, and temperature increases of more than 5.4°F (3°C) would significantly alter production of all food crops.

According to *Climate Change 2007*, the Fourth Assessment Report of the United Nations' Intergovernmental Panel on Climate Change (IPCC), a scientific body charged by the United Nations with summarizing the best climate science, even small temperature increases (1.8°F–3.6°F or 1°C–2°C) will result in decreases in crop productivity in many dry and tropical regions. In the areas that already have a semiarid climate, crops will be negatively affected by more frequent droughts and floods resulting from global warming as well as by a decrease in water available for irrigation. At the same time, in more temperate areas of the world, the increased carbon in the atmosphere and extended growing seasons caused by global warming could result in a slight increase in crop productivity, as long as local temperatures do not rise too greatly. Larger temperature increases, however, will significantly decrease crop production even in temperate regions, the IPCC predicts.

The IPCC warns that, on a global scale, average temperature increases beyond 1.8°F–3.6°F (1°C–2°C) threaten crop production of the world's major food grains—wheat, rice, corn, soybeans, barley, and sorghum—and temperature increases of more than 5.4°F (3°C) would significantly alter production of all food crops. The 2007 IPCC report projects warming of between

2°F and 11.5°F (1.1°C and 5.4°C) by the end of the twenty-first century, so these predictions of global crop losses could come to pass.

Various studies echo the IPCC's findings about crop losses and add to concerns about global food security—that is, whether people around the world will have access to a sufficient amount of safe and nutritious food. A 2009 report from the International Food Policy Research Institute (IFPRI), a Washington, D.C.– based anti-hunger organization, for example, found that climate change is likely to create a worldwide agricultural and food crisis. IFPRI agricultural economist Gerald Nelson, the author of the report, has explained:

> Higher temperatures and changes in precipitation result in pressure on yields from important crops in much of the world. . . . Biological impacts on crop yields work through the economic system resulting in reduced production, higher crop and meat prices, and a reduction in cereal consumption. This reduction means reduced calorie intake and increased childhood malnutrition.[2]

The impact of global warming, however, will vary from country to country and among different regions of the world. Developing countries are likely to be the hardest hit. The IPCC report, for example, warns that Africa and parts of Asia are two of the most vulnerable regions because of multiple climate stresses. Similarly, the IFPRI report projects that wheat yields could fall at least 20 percent, with many of the worst losses in parts of sub-Saharan Africa and South Asia. Agricultural production is also expected to decline in southern and eastern Australia.

In the United States, however, the IPCC predicts that moderate climate change, which could mean increased amounts of rainfall for many parts of the country, may actually increase yields of rain-fed agriculture by 5 to 20 percent. Yet even in North America, there are some areas that will suffer. The western United States, in particular, will be affected because warming will reduce the snowpack in the Sierra Mountains—one of the main sources of water for California and other southwestern states. The IPCC says that these mountain snow resources could eventually be reduced by 60 to 90 percent—a change that may deprive farmers in California's famous Central Valley farm region of irrigation water in the summers. Other areas of the country also could be negatively affected. Experts say grazing lands for cattle in such places as Colorado could become less nutritious because of drier conditions, and citrus groves in Florida could be damaged by increased rainstorms and hurricanes. The vast midwestern Corn Belt—a region known for its production of corn for human food, animal feed, and biofuel energy—could even dry up and lose the ability to produce corn crops.

Climate Changes So Far

Climate changes are already being seen around the world. Recent U.S. government reports note a number of signs that point to long-term climate change in the United States. For example, the U.S. average temperature has risen more than 2°F (1.1°C) over the past fifty years while overall precipitation has increased by about 5 percent in that same time period. In some areas, such as the Midwest, average temperatures have increased as much as 7°F (3.9°C). In addition, extreme weather events such as heat waves, droughts, and heavy downpours have become more frequent; Atlantic hurricanes have become more intense; sea levels have risen; Alaska's arctic sea ice is rapidly melting; and the Sierra snowpack has been slowly but steadily decreasing for many decades.

Similar warming effects have been documented in the rest of the world. Temperature records show that global average surface temperatures—the temperatures of the air near the surface of the earth—have risen substantially since 1970, and this warming trend is confirmed by changes such as the retreat of mountain glaciers, melting of arctic sea ice, reductions in snow cover, earlier blooming of plants in spring, and increased melting of the Greenland and antarctic ice sheets. Changes in precipitation have also been observed, with some regions experiencing more rain and flooding and others facing droughts. Meanwhile, sea levels around the world have risen about 8 inches (20.32 cm) over the past hundred years. Experts think these climate changes have already begun to affect global agricultural production and that the future holds more of the same. According to Joachim von Braun, director general of IFPRI, the world was given a taste of this future when wheat and corn production declined by 12 to 16 percent between 2004 and 2006 in both the United States and Europe, due largely to adverse weather and reduced plantings. These and other factors, such as growth in demand for food and rising energy prices, produced volatile and drastic spikes in food prices—impacts that may become common with higher temperatures.

All of the reported changes conform to climate models used by scientists to predict the effects of global warming, and in some cases the changes have occurred faster than scientists had predicted. Unless humans act to cut greenhouse gases emissions, climate experts say the earth will continue to warm, producing more climate changes that could disrupt, reduce, or even destroy farm production in many parts of the globe.

Agriculture's Contribution to Global Warming

Not only has farming been affected by today's global warming crisis; it has also contributed to it. According to a 2009 report by the independent research group Worldwatch Institute, "more than 30 percent of all greenhouse gas emissions arise from the land use sector,"[3] which the group defines as crop farming, livestock grazing, and deforestation—the cutting down of forests to create agricultural land for growing crops or grazing animals. The IPCC estimates that agriculture alone, not including issues relating to forests, accounts for 10–12 percent of global greenhouse gases.

Most of these agriculture emissions, environmental activists say, are caused by our system of modern industrialized agricul-

Modern industrial farming techniques such as high-volume livestock production and the use of nitrogen fertilizers contribute to global warming. AP Images/Timothy Jacobsen.

ture, which employs massive amounts of chemical fertilizers and raises animals in highly concentrated facilities. Nitrogen fertilizers, for example, produce one of the most powerful greenhouse gases—nitrous oxide (N_2O)—and also pollute groundwater and waterways. Animal production is another large emitter of greenhouse gases; livestock such as beef and dairy cattle emit large amounts of methane, another potent greenhouse gas, through their digestive process, and the rising global demand for meat makes its production a growing source of harmful emissions. Deforestation, too, is a huge contributor to greenhouse gas emissions because it removes trees, plants, and soils that act as "carbon sinks," which extract carbon dioxide from the atmosphere. Experts are most concerned about deforestation in developing countries, many of which have some of the world's last remaining rainforests.

The Future Role of Agriculture

Because it is both implicated in and affected by global warming, climate experts say agriculture must play a significant role in responding to these various climate threats. A number of experts, for example, recommend embracing more sustainable farming practices in order to improve the resiliency of the global agriculture system in the face of climate change and to reduce greenhouse emissions. Various strategies have been proposed to help the industry mitigate, or lessen the impact of, global warming, and to adapt to changes that have already begun. Many such strategies are concerned with carbon sequestration—keeping carbon in the soil. One popular method is no-till farming, a technique of avoiding plowing or disturbing the soil and simply planting new crops amid the debris of previous crops. Other agricultural strategies include introducing drought-resistant and weed-resistant crop varieties, reducing the intensive use of chemical fertilizers and pesticides, improving water conservation, and improving grasslands and livestock management.

Ultimately, agricultural experts hope that implementing new ways of growing food and other products will help to create both a more sustainable agricultural system and a cooler, cleaner world while still maintaining or increasing farm yields. Achieving these goals will be difficult but the incentive to succeed is great. As Australian scientist Mark Howden argues, "We will need to think about smart ways of feeding the world. . . . We are looking at a requirement to double agricultural production by 2050, so this isn't the time when we have the luxury of cutting back our agriculture. We're on a treadmill [and] we need to keeping running faster and faster."[4]

Notes

1. Quoted in Ian Sample, "World Faces 'Perfect Storm' of Problems by 2030, Chief Scientist to Warn," *The Guardian*, March 18, 2009. www.guardian.co.uk.
2. Quoted in David Biello, "Farmed Out: How Will Climate Change Impact World Food Supplies?" *Scientific American*, September 30, 2009. www.scientificamerican.com.
3. Sara J. Scherr and Sajal Sthapit, "Mitigating Climate Change Through Food and Land Use, Summary," Worldwatch Institute, 2009. www.worldwatch.org.
4. Quoted in Reuters, "Climate Change Will Harm Farmers," May 4, 2008. http://tvnz .co.nz.

CHAPTER 2

Impact on Crops from Changes in Temperature, Precipitation, and Carbon Dioxide

According to the Intergovernmental Panel on Climate Change (IPCC), 40 percent of the earth's land surface is used for cropland and pasture, and the agricultural sector is a fundamental industry in the economies of both developed and developing nations. Agriculture is especially important in developing countries, where almost 70 percent of people live in rural areas dependent on agricultural jobs and where agriculture is the main engine of economic growth. According to scientists, however, the future may bring climate changes, including more extreme weather events, changes in temperature and precipitation, and elevated levels of carbon dioxide (CO_2) in the atmosphere. These changes, when combined, could threaten historically stable agricultural areas and world food crop production.

Unpredictable Weather

The IPCC says that some of the worst climate impacts for crops will be severe variations in weather that will mean less predictability for farmers around the globe. The 2007 IPCC report predicts that it is "very likely" (which the IPCC defines as a 90 percent chance) the world will see an increased number of various extreme weather events in the coming century. Examples of extreme weather include more frequent and severe heat and cold waves, storm activity of greater intensity, heavy precipitation, high winds, longer droughts, stronger cyclones and hurricanes, more widespread flooding, and larger wildfires.

Scientists say that the world is already experiencing some of these effects. James McCarthy, a professor of biological oceanography at Harvard University, for example, points to events such as Hurricane Mitch, which killed nearly eleven thousand people in Central America in 1998; flooding in Bangladesh in 1999; and a record heat wave that hit Europe in 2003. As McCarthy explains, "Weather records are being set all the time now. We're in an era of unprecedented extreme weather events."[1] Indeed, according to a 2008 report by the Food and Agriculture Organization of the United Nations, "An average of 500 weather-related disasters are now taking place each year, compared with 120 in the 1980s; the number of floods has increased sixfold over the same period. Population increases, especially in coastal areas, where most of the world's population now lives, mean that more and more people will be affected by catastrophic weather events."[2]

The 2007 IPCC report makes specific predictions about the effect of these extreme weather events on crops, indicating that more frequent extreme weather events could lower crop yields beyond the levels previously projected. For example, crops might be damaged if severe weather hits at critical times, such as during plant flowering or just before harvest time. Similarly, unpredictable weather might make applications of fertilizers or other farm inputs more difficult and cause other types of damage that could stunt plant growth and yields.

A number of simulation studies cited by the IPCC support this finding of heightened danger to crops from an increase in extreme weather episodes. A 2002 study, for example, found that increased heavy rainfall caused by climate changes in the United States may double U.S. corn production losses by 2030, which could cost farmers as much as $3 billion per year. Another study found that other factors related to unpredictable weather could further increase crop losses. Higher levels of salinization (that is, salt), for example, could develop in soils in more arid regions because of water loss from drought conditions or rising sea levels. The 2007 report concludes—with a high level of confidence—that "projected changes in the frequency and severity of extreme climate events will have more serious consequences for food and . . . food insecurity, than will changes in . . . temperature and precipitation."[3]

Changes in Temperature and Precipitation

Although severe weather events may have more dramatic consequences, temperature and rainfall changes caused by global

Extreme rainfall poses dangers to corn crops and may increase losses to $3 billion per year by 2030. © Kim Karpeles/Alamy.

The 2003 European Heat Wave

Many scientists point to a record heat wave that struck Europe in 2003 as one example of the kind of extreme weather events that could become more common in the future as a result of global warming. The unusually hot weather arrived in June 2003 and culminated in a blistering two weeks in August, when temperatures hovered around 104°F (40°C), during both the daytime and at night. Weather experts say that August 2003 was the hottest August on record in the northern hemisphere.

The heat dried up rivers, fueled fires, and caused European crop yields to drop significantly. The heat wave also had a dramatic impact on human health: Hospitals were inundated, and tens of thousands of people died. Initially, reports stated that 35,000 deaths were attributable to the heat, but according to a 2006 report by the environmental group Earth Policy Institute, later information revealed that more than 52,000 Europeans died. France led with the most heat-related deaths, but Germany, Spain, Italy, Portugal, and the United Kingdom also reported high death figures. High temperatures can be deadly to humans because the body must struggle to maintain a healthy body temperature of 98.6°F (55°C) by sweating and pumping blood closer to the skin. High heat, particularly when constant through day and night and when combined with high humidity, can overwhelm the body's cooling mechanisms and result in death. The elderly and the infirm are most at risk.

warming could also negatively affect global crop production. As the IPCC 2007 report explains, for many food crops, including grains, hot or cold temperatures at critical times (such as during flowering periods) can diminish both the size and quality of the crop or even cause plant death. Similarly, warmer temperatures and droughts during extended growing periods can also cause faster evaporation of water from the soil and leave plants parched—a scenario that could significantly diminish crop yields and quality.

In addition, because more than 80 percent of total agricultural land is watered by rainfall, changes in precipitation will often affect future crop production regardless of other positive growing conditions. For crops that are artificially irrigated, rising temperatures can increase crops' requirements for irrigation. A 2006 study mentioned in the IPCC report, for example, found that global irrigation requirements could increase by 20 percent by 2080, with larger increases in developed countries, due to both increased evaporation and longer growing seasons caused by climate change in these regions. Increased water stress is also predicted for other irrigated regions of the world, such as the Middle East, Southeast Asia, and North Africa.

In some more temperate regions, however, warmer temperatures will extend growing seasons, possibly increasing crop production. The U.S. Climate Change Science Program, a project launched by President George W. Bush, reported in 2008 that the growing season has already increased by ten to fourteen days in northern parts of the United States over the last nineteen years.

Rising Carbon Dioxide Levels

Another of the climate changes predicted by scientists is ever-increasing levels of carbon dioxide in the earth's atmosphere. Because carbon dioxide (CO_2) is used by plants as part of photosynthesis—the process by which plants use sunlight to convert carbon dioxide into food—rising CO_2 concentrations that contribute to the global warming process could actually improve crop growth and production. This process is called carbon fertilization. Today, the amount of CO_2 in the atmosphere is approximately 380 parts per million (ppm)—that is, 380 units of carbon dioxide for every million units of air in the earth's atmosphere. According to the 2007 IPCC report, experimental studies have shown that many plants, without considering other effects of climate change, will respond positively to higher levels of CO_2. Recent analyses, for example, have found that under unstressed conditions, increases in CO_2 atmospheric concentrations to 550 ppm increase crop yields in the range of 10–20 percent for some crops (such as wheat) and 0–10 percent for other crops (such as corn).

Increases in plant growth and yield because of high CO_2 levels, however, will vary depending on the species, growth stage, availability of water, nitrogen fertilizer applications, and other factors. Results could also be less positive under actual field conditions, where plants may face threats such as pests, weeds, and competition from other plants. In addition, future climate changes such as higher temperatures and reduced rainfall are likely to further limit the positive effects of high CO_2 levels. For example, the IPCC explains that "rain-fed wheat grown at 450 ppm CO_2 demonstrated yield increases with temperature increases of up to [1.44°F or 0.8°C] . . . but [yield] declines with temperature increases beyond [2.7°F or 1.5°C]. . . ."[4] The bottom line is that scientists cannot be completely certain at this point what the actual effects will be on world crops from the combination of both damaging and beneficial projected climate changes.

Global Food Crop Production

According to the 2007 IPCC report, the effect of climate changes on global food crop productivity also depends on exactly how much average temperatures rise in coming decades. The IPCC concludes that world agriculture may benefit if temperatures increase slightly, but significantly higher temperatures pose a threat to crop production.

'Globally, the potential for food production is projected to increase with increases in local average temperature over a range of 1–3°C, but above this it is projected to decrease.'

More specifically, the IPCC projects that relatively small local temperature increases of 1.8°F to 5.4°F (1°C to 3°C) in regions that lie in mid to high latitudes—places such as northern Europe,

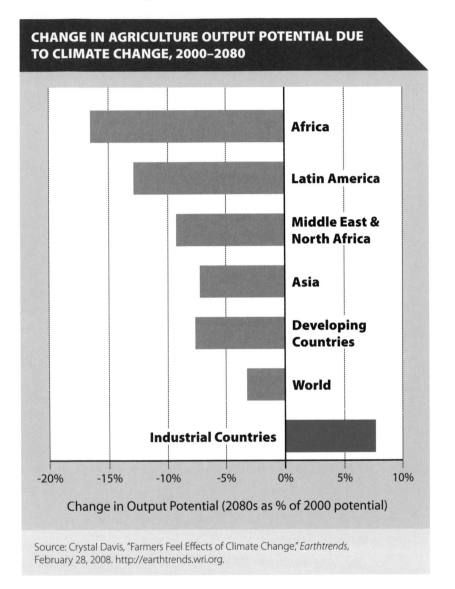

CHANGE IN AGRICULTURE OUTPUT POTENTIAL DUE TO CLIMATE CHANGE, 2000–2080

Africa

Latin America

Middle East & North Africa

Asia

Developing Countries

World

Industrial Countries

-20%   -15%   -10%   -5%   0%   5%   10%

Change in Output Potential (2080s as % of 2000 potential)

Source: Crystal Davis, "Farmers Feel Effects of Climate Change," *Earthtrends*, February 28, 2008. http://earthtrends.wri.org.

North America, New Zealand, and parts of Latin America—might be beneficial because warmer temperatures will prolong growing seasons, and higher CO_2 levels might aid plant growth. At temperatures above this range, however, the IPCC predicts that crop production will decrease in these areas. At lower latitudes, especially in seasonally dry areas and tropical regions close to the equator, the IPCC report says crop productivity will decrease even with slight temperature increases. Many of these parts of the world already have a semiarid climate, so crops in these regions will also be negatively affected by other aspects of climate change, such as extreme weather and water shortages.

Because much of the world's food grain supply is now produced in these low-latitude and mid- to high-latitude countries (rather than in low- to mid-latitude countries), the IPCC concludes that global grain production could be threatened as local average temperatures in these areas rise during coming decades, and that the global grain system can accommodate an increase of no more than 5.4°F (3°C) before declining. If local average temperatures increase more than 5.4°F (3°C), all crops in all regions could be affected, the IPCC says. The IPCC summarizes these findings as follows: "Globally, the potential for food production is projected to increase with increases in local average temperature over a range of 1–3°C, but above this it is projected to decrease."[5] Writer Dan Charles has described what this scenario means in the near term for food production, explaining:

> Most scientists don't foresee major changes in total food production during the next decade or two, as average temperatures increase by just a few degrees. On average, across the globe, the positive effects of more carbon dioxide in the atmosphere are projected to cancel out the negative effects caused by rising temperatures. Even during this period, though, some regions will benefit and others will lose ground. Food production is projected to increase in temperate regions, such as North America and Europe. It may fall, however, in sub-Saharan Africa or India. As a result, the world will become increasingly dependent on a handful of major food exporters, such as the United States, Canada, Australia, Brazil and Argentina.[6]

Scientists agree that the earth will continue to warm throughout this century, so it is probable that crop production will decline. The 2007 IPCC report, for example, predicts an additional warming of between 3.1°F and 7.2°F (1.7°C and 4°C) by the end of the century, and many climate experts are now predicting that average global temperatures could rise even faster. A 2009 report from the United Kingdom's Met Office Hadley Centre for Climate Prediction and Research, for example, found that average global temperatures could rise by 7.2°F (4°C) as early as 2060 if humans fail to reduce emissions. A 2009 study conducted by Robert Corell, chair of the Climate Action Initiative, with climate researchers at the Sustainability Institute, Ventana Systems, and the Massachusetts Institute of Technology, projected a 6.3°F (3.5°C) temperature increase by the end of the century—even if countries followed through on the most aggressive emissions reductions proposals. As Richard Betts, head of climate impacts at the Hadley Centre, has explained, "These [warming] impacts will have very large consequences for food security, water availability and health."[7]

Climate Impacts on Industrial Crops

Although there is a growing body of research on the effects of climate changes upon primary food crops such as wheat and other grains, according to the 2007 IPCC report very few studies have been done to measure climate impacts on industrial crops. Examples of industrial crops include oilseeds (plants grown for their oils—such as flax, sunflowers, and groundnuts including peanuts); gums and resins; food sweeteners; beverages (like coffee and tea); fibers (grown to make paper, cloth, or rope); and medicinal and aromatic plants. The limited research available indicates that these crops are likely to suffer the same overall fate that food crops do as climate changes occur, however. A study conducted in 2002 of the effects of reduced rainfall on groundnut crops in Niger, a large groundnut producer and exporter, found that production would decrease by 11 to 25 percent. Similarly, though increased levels of CO_2 have been found to increase cotton crop yields in simulated studies, yields decreased when changes in temperature and precipitation were factored into the studies. As a result, scientists have predicted a 9 percent loss in future years in fiber yields for the Mississippi Delta, a large cotton-growing region in the southern United States.

Another category of industrial crops—biofuels—is also likely to be affected by climate changes. Biofuel crops such as corn and sugar beets could benefit from increased CO_2 levels in regions such as North America and Europe, as long as temperatures do not rise too high and sufficient rainfall is available. In addition, switchgrass—a perennial warm season biofuel crop—has shown yield increases under climate change conditions. Like food crops and other industrial crops, however, many biofuel crop yields may decrease or vary season by season if hit with higher temperatures or droughts.

The 2007 IPCC report concluded that climate change could cause greater harm to perennial industrial crops than to annual crops, because both damage from global warming (such as extreme weather events or changes in temperature and rainfall) and benefits from it (such as increased levels of CO_2 and longer growing seasons) may accumulate over time. An example of this phenomenon is a series of cyclones that struck parts of India in 1952, 1955, 1996, and 1998; each of these storms destroyed so many slow-growing coconut palms that it took and is taking years to restore production to previous levels. All forms of crop farming, therefore, are likely to be significantly affected by coming changes in climate.

Notes

1. Quoted in Stephen Leahy, "Global Warming May Spawn More Super-Storms," *Inter Press Service*, September 20, 2004. www.ipsnews.net.
2. Food and Agriculture Organization of the United Nations, "Climate Change and Food Security: A Framework Document," 2008, p. 20. www.fao.org.
3. Intergovernmental Panel on Climate Change (IPCC), "Chapter 5: Food, Fibre and Forest Products," in *Climate Change 2007: Impacts, Adaptation and Vulnerability, Contribution of Working Group II to the Fourth Assessment Report*, M.L. Parry, O.F. Canziani, J.P. Palutikof, P.J. van der Linden, and C.E. Hanson, New York: Cambridge University Press, 2008, p. 299. www.ipcc.ch.

4. IPCC, "Chapter 5: Food, Fibre and Forest Products," p. 282.
5. IPCC, "Summary for Policymakers," in *Climate Change 2007: Impacts, Adaptation and Vulnerability,* p. 11.
6. Dan Charles, "Will a Warmer World Have Enough Food?" NPR, October 29, 2007. www.npr.org.
7. Quoted in Kate Sheppard, "Report Predicts 7.3 Degree Temperature Rise by 2060," *Mother Jones*, September 28, 2009. http://motherjones.com.

CHAPTER 3

Concerns About Water, Soil, and Pests

Water and arable land (terrain that is suitable for cultivation) are vital for a flourishing global agriculture system. In fact, according to the United Nations Intergovernmental Panel on Climate Change (IPCC), almost 70 percent of human water withdrawals from freshwater sources such as rivers, lakes, and below-ground aquifers is dedicated to the irrigation of crops. In recent decades, global water use has increased because of population growth, economic expansion in developing nations, and related matters. Also, according to the IPCC, as temperatures rise and rainfall decreases, water use typically increases, mostly because farmers need more water for irrigation. In many parts of the world, therefore, a warmer climate will lead to greater demand for freshwater. Much of the world already suffers from a lack of water resources, however, and global warming is expected to exacerbate this situation. Climate changes such as rising temperatures and decreasing rainfall may also cause soil erosion and desertification (the transformation of habitable, agricultural land to desert) in certain regions, along with a proliferation of crop pests, diseases, and weeds. These secondary climate impacts could further hinder world agriculture and food production in coming decades.

Changes in Water Availability

According to the 2007 IPCC report, climate changes are likely to affect water availability in severe and adverse ways. Contributing

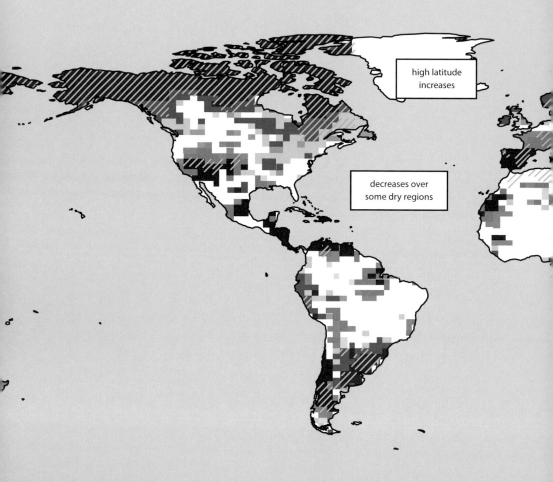

high latitude
increases

decreases over
some dry regions

Source: Intergovernmental Panel on Climate Change, *Climate Change 2007: Synthesis Report: Contribution of Working Groups I, II and III to the Fourth Assessment Report of the Intergovernmental Panel on Climate Change*, edited by R.K. Pachauri and A. Reisinger, Geneva, Switzerland: IPCC, p. 49.

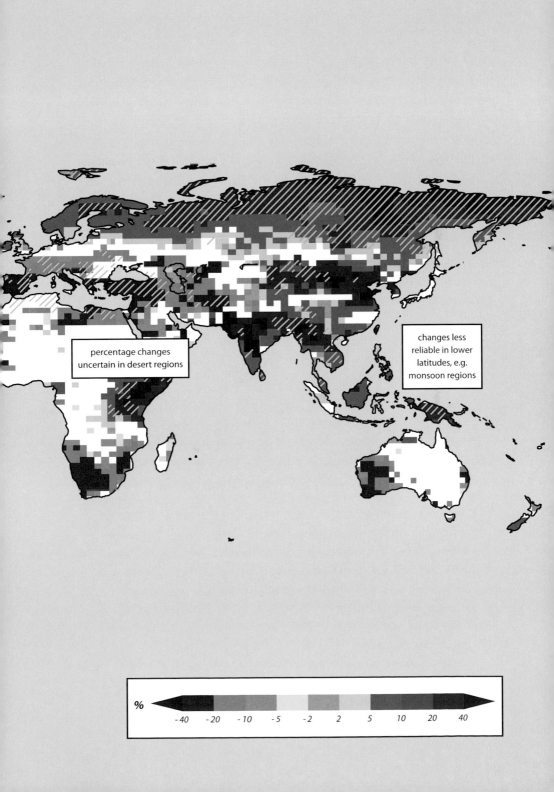

percentage changes
uncertain in desert regions

changes less
reliable in lower
latitudes, e.g.
monsoon regions

%   - 40   - 20   - 10   - 5   - 2   2   5   10   20   40

climate factors include changes in precipitation, temperature, and rates of evaporation (which are affected by other factors such as humidity, wind, and temperature). Impacts on water resources will vary from one location to the next. Some regions, for example, are dependent on snowmelt or glacier melt to provide water for streams, lakes, and wells, and high temperatures in some of these areas could lead to less snow in the winters and, thus, reduced stream flow and a decreased water supply in summers. In fact, according to the World Wildlife Fund, an environmental group, 67 percent of the world's glaciers are already melting and "up to a quarter of the global mountain glacier mass could disappear by 2050 and up to half could be lost by 2100."[1] In semiarid areas, warmer temperatures are likely to result in decreased rainfall levels, extending the dry season and producing less water for precious reservoirs and deep groundwater wells. Some low-lying coastal areas could also be negatively affected, as rising sea levels caused by global warming invade fresh groundwater and estuaries. Sea levels are expected to rise as a result of thermal expansion of the ocean, as well as melting glaciers and ice sheets. At the same time, other parts of the world may receive more rainfall than in the past—a climate impact that could cause flooding of farms and croplands. The 2007 IPCC report summarizes these water-related climate impacts as follows:

> By mid-century, annual average river runoff and water availability are projected to increase by 10–40% at high latitudes and in some wet tropical areas, and decrease by 10–30% over some dry regions at mid-latitudes and in the dry tropics, some of which are presently water-stressed areas. . . . Drought-affected areas will likely increase in extent. Heavy precipitation events, which are very likely to increase in frequency, will augment flood risk. . . . Water supplies stored in glaciers and snow cover are projected to decline, reducing water availability in regions supplied by meltwater from major mountain ranges."[2]

Although some areas will see benefits, the overall impact of climate change on global freshwater resources will be detrimental. As the IPCC explains, "The negative impacts of climate change on freshwater systems outweigh its benefits."[3]

'By mid-century, annual average river runoff and water availability are projected to . . . decrease by 10-30% over some dry regions at mid-latitudes and in the dry tropics, some of which are presently water-stressed areas.'

Decreasing water supplies caused by global warming will affect millions of people around the world. Climate scientists say that more than one sixth of the world's population lives in regions where water supplies are fed by melting glaciers or mountain snow. In the Andes mountain range in South America, for example, glacial meltwater supports river flow and water supply for tens of millions of people in countries such as Bolivia, Ecuador, and Peru. Similarly, the Hindu Kush mountain range, which runs for 500 miles between northwestern Pakistan and eastern and central Afghanistan, and the Himalayas, which provide water to hundreds of millions of people in China and India, will be negatively affected. Many coastal regions are densely populated and will be increasingly affected by salinization of their water resources, a likely result of rising sea levels. It is the semiarid and arid areas, however, that will be most exposed to negative climate impacts on freshwater, according to the IPCC. These areas, which already suffer from a lack of water, include the Mediterranean basin, the western United States, parts of Africa, and northeastern Brazil.

The IPCC also predicts that many aspects of climate change, such as warmer water temperatures, severe storms, and longer periods of low water flows in rivers and streams, will exacerbate water pollution. And the stress of climate changes will only add to other impacts—such as population growth, economic development, and urbanization—which already adversely affect freshwater systems. Together, these stresses will force water managers to incorporate new strategies, such as greater reuse of wastewater, into their plans.

Floods and Droughts

In some areas climate impacts could be extensive, producing severe droughts or floods that are expected to significantly hurt local crop production. Scientists say flooding of rivers and other areas could be caused by intense or prolonged rainfall or snow, as well as snowmelt, dam breaks, and ice jams or landslides across waterways. In areas that are considered to be hundred-year-flood zones, the IPCC predicts that floods could instead occur every two to five years.

In addition to occurring more frequently, flooding will also be widespread; the IPCC's 2007 report projects that "up to 20% of the world population will live in areas where river flood potential could increase by the 2080s."[4] In other areas, droughts may develop because of below-average precipitation, low soil moisture, or low water levels in rivers, lakes, and groundwater systems. Droughts could also occur in some areas because precipitation will come in the form of rain rather than snow, thus reducing snowpack levels and producing droughts in late summer, when demand for water is at its highest. Because precipitation is predicted to increase significantly at mid and high latitudes, such areas are where flood risks will be highest, while droughts are most likely over low latitudes and mid latitudes during summer months.

One of the areas expected to be affected by both these phenomena is Europe. In northern Europe the IPCC predicts there will be more frequent floods, but in southern Europe there will be a decrease in summer precipitation and rising temperatures that will enhance evaporation, reduce summer soil moisture, and ultimately result in more frequent and more intense droughts. Developing countries, however, may suffer the most from cli-

Global Warming Changes in the Nile River Delta

According to the World Bank, a United Nations agency created to help developing nations by providing loans, Egypt may face severe water impacts from climate change. The country's Nile River delta—a large area of rich, cultivated land at the mouth of the Nile River, where it meets the Mediterranean Sea—is vulnerable to flooding and salinization as the Mediterranean Sea rises because of global warming. This area is home to 80 million people and produces almost half of Egypt's food crops, including wheat, bananas, and rice. Scientists have predicted that the Mediterranean, like other seas around the world, will rise between 1 foot and 3.3 feet (0.3 to 1 m) by the end of this century—a phenomenon that could flood coastal areas, force more than 10 percent of Egyptians from their homes, and destroy essential food supplies. The seawater would also contaminate the freshwater in the Nile River, which is widely used for irrigation. In a worst-case scenario in which global warming causes a rapid breakup of the Greenland and West Antarctica ice sheets, the ocean could potentially rise by about 16 feet (5 m). For Egypt, this change would truly be catastrophic. Already, experts say that the Mediterranean has risen between 0.1 and 0.4 inches (2.5 and 10 mm) per year since the 1990s and flooded parts of its coastal regions.

mate extremes. For example, climate experts say that Bangladesh, one of the world's poorest countries, may be hit by a 23–29 percent increase in flooding, assuming global temperatures rise by 3.6°F (2°C).

Overall, however, climate experts expect more drought than flooding. The IPCC predicts, for example, "that the proportion of the land surface in extreme drought, globally, [will] increase by a factor of 10 to 30; from 1–3% for the present day to 30% by the 2090s."[5] Africa, many parts of which routinely experience severe drought conditions, may be most at risk for drier conditions. Africa has a history of long droughts, including a decade-long drought that began in the 1960s in the region of Sahel—a section across central Africa that includes the countries of Sudan, Niger, Chad, Mali, and Mauretania—that killed about one hundred thousand people. According to recent research, climate change could bring even more of these types of deadly droughts to West Africa and make them even hotter and of longer duration.

Desertification, Erosion, and Soil Losses

The 2007 IPCC report also concludes that climate change will have negative effects on soils, in some areas causing drying that could turn productive farmlands into deserts—a process called desertification—and in other areas causing soil erosion, or loss of soil. As is the case with many other climate impacts, however, certain areas (such as Russia) may benefit because they could gain arable land as temperatures rise and once freezing regions become more temperate in climate.

Desertification can result from an interplay of multiple climate changes, including higher temperatures, decreased rainfall, more intense droughts, increased solar radiation, and stronger winds. Desertification of soil, in turn, releases CO_2 as vegetation dies or is cleared from dry lands, and desertified land also absorbs less carbon from the atmosphere because it contains less plant life—both processes that add to the global warming trend. Already, some arid and semiarid areas in countries such as Spain and Kazakhstan have begun to experience these changes, as reduced rainfall has caused croplands to be abandoned in recent years. As Yvo de Boer, secretary of the United Nations Framework Convention on Climate Change, has explained, "Climate change has become the prime cause of an accelerating spread of deserts which threatens the world's drylands."[6] In the future, de Boer says, major deserts such as the Sahara, Gobi, and Kalahari will expand and as many as one hundred countries could be at risk of

Once fertile areas such as Riganqiao Swamp in China's Sichuan province have undergone desertification, prompting former croplands to be abandoned. AP Images/Li Jiacheng/Color China Photo.

desertification. Threatened countries include Australia and the United States, where desertification could occur in parts of the American Southwest, including California.

Increases in rainfall or snowfall amounts and in the intensity of storms in other regions, on the other hand, can lead to soil erosion because water has the power to wash away topsoils. One of the most important climate drivers of erosion is the expected change from snowfall to rainfall in many areas of the world, especially northern regions. There, warmer winter temperatures are expected to bring rain instead of snow, and rainfall is much more destructive to soils than snow. In some areas, too, soils may become more susceptible to erosion because of climate changes that reduce the amount of plant canopy and mulch that protects the organic matter in the soil. In colder regions, the melting of permafrost—frozen subsoils—could also create areas more likely to erode during rainstorms. Studies have shown that rainfall erosion is already happening and in the future could be quite significant in certain areas. For example, a 2005 study to assess erosion in the Yellow River basin in China—a region where erosion rates are currently extremely high—projected future erosion increases of 8 to 30 percent by 2080.[7] Similarly, a 2002 simulation of increased rainfall in eight corn- and wheat-growing locations in the United States found that significant escalations in precipitation produce even higher rates of erosion—results indicating that climate change in the coming century will have a notable impact on erosion.[8]

Climate Impacts on Pests, Diseases, and Weeds

Climate changes are likely to increase the threats to crops from pests, plant diseases, and weeds, too. The 2007 IPCC report notes, for instance, that "recent warming trends in the U.S. and Canada have led to earlier spring activity of insects and proliferation of some species, such as the mountain pine beetle."[9] In addition, studies predict that swings in climate conditions, such as warmer temperatures in temperate regions such as the United States and Europe, could allow insects from the tropics to migrate northward, infecting food crops and bringing disease and possibly death to both wildlife and humans. Studies have also suggested that climate change can increase the range and severity of plant diseases and invasive species in future years. An April 2010 report by the National Wildlife Federation, for example, listed seven pests and invasive plants—deer tick, poison ivy, fire ant, Asian tiger mosquito, cheatgrass, saltcedar, and pine bark beetle—that are likely to expand their range, increase their numbers, or become more toxic because of warmer temperatures and climate change.

Similarly, increased CO_2 levels and increases in rainfall in some areas could help weeds to grow. Recent studies by ecologist Lewis Ziska of the Agriculture Research Service of the

U.S. Department of Agriculture, for example, demonstrate that warmer temperatures and higher levels of CO_2 caused weeds to grow faster and bigger and to produce more pollen. In fact, over a period of five growing seasons, Ziska grew superweeds that were almost twice as large as normal and with double the amount of pollen, simply by enriching levels of CO_2 in a city plot of land in Baltimore, Maryland. Ziska's studies and similar ones suggest that weeds, because of their genetic diversity, will flourish more than crops in a warming climate. As Ziska has explained, "When you change a resource in the environment, you are going to, in effect, favor the weed over the crop. There is always going to be a weed poised genetically to benefit from almost any change."[10] Prolific weed growth could pose yet another new obstacle to crop production in coming years.

The direct consequences of climate change—rising temperatures, changes in rainfall, and increased CO_2—will thus produce a variety of secondary impacts on crops that will make farming much more challenging in the twenty-first century.

Notes

1. World Wildlife Fund, "An Overview of Glaciers, Glacier Retreat, and Subsequent Impacts in Nepal, India and China," March 2005. www.wwfnepal.org.
2. Intergovernmental Panel on Climate Change (IPCC), "Summary for Policymakers," in *Climate Change 2007: Impacts, Adaptation and Vulnerability: Contribution of Working Group II to the Fourth Assessment Report*, eds. M.L. Parry, O.F. Canziani, J.P. Palutikof, P.J. van der Linden, and C.E. Hanson, New York: Cambridge University Press, 2008, p. 11. www.ipcc.ch.
3. IPCC, "Chapter 3: Freshwater Resources and Their Management ," in *Climate Change 2007: Impacts, Adaptation and Vulnerability*, p. 175.
4. IPCC, "Synthesis Report," in *Climate Change 2007: Impacts, Adaptation and Vulnerability,* p. 49.
5. IPCC, "Chapter 3: Freshwater Resources and Their Management ," p. 187.
6. Quoted in Joseph Romm, "Desertification Amplifies Climate Change," *Grist*, September 13, 2007. www.grist.org.
7. M.A. Zhang, G. Nearing, B. Liu, "Potential Effects of Climate Change on Rainfall Erosivity in the Yellow River Basin of China," *Transactions of the American Society of Agricultural Engineers*, vol. 48, 2005, pp. 511–517. www.ars.usda.gov.
8. F.F. Pruski and M.A. Nearing, "Climate-Induced Changes in Erosion During the 21st Century for Eight U.S. Locations," *Water Resources Research*, vol. 38, 2002, p. 1298. http://ddr.nal.usda.gov.

9. IPCC, "Chapter 5: Food, Fibre and Forest Products," in *Climate Change 2007: Impacts, Adaptation and Vulnerability*, p. 283.
10. Quoted in Kimberley D. Mok, "USDA Study: Climate Change Could Benefit Super Weeds More Than Crops," *TreeHugger*, June 30, 2008. www.treehugger.com.

CHAPTER 4

Impact of Global Warming on Livestock, Dairy, and Fish Production

Climate changes not only threaten global crop production; they could also affect the economic viability of livestock, dairy, and fish production systems around the world. According to climate experts, animal producers who graze cattle, dairy cows, or other animals in outdoor pastures could see decreases in the quality of grasses and forage plants because of more challenging growing conditions and the invasion of grasslands by inedible or lower-protein types of vegetation. Animal producers, both those who graze their animals and those who raise animals in confined animal operations, can also expect to face production declines because of the additional stress that hotter temperatures will create for the animals—heat stress that can lead to decreased feeding and milk production. Extreme weather events—such as unexpected heat waves, frigid temperatures, thunderstorms, and snowstorms—pose further serious challenges and can even cause animal deaths. Experts say many of the same climate changes that affect land animals could also spell trouble for fish. All of these impacts on production, experts predict, could translate into higher meat, dairy, and fish prices in the future.

Changes in Pasturelands and Rangelands

The United Nations Intergovernmental Panel on Climate Change (IPCC) projects that climate changes such as increases in CO_2

Global Warming Challenges for U.S. Western Rangelands

Beef cattle are produced throughout the United States, but eastern pasturelands are generally seeded by farmers while western rangelands, which tend to be much drier, rely on wild, native grasses and plants. These arid western rangelands are expected to be more affected by future climate changes. Today, western grasses are already under stress because of warming temperatures, reduced rainfall, rising levels of carbon dioxide (CO_2), and invasion by woody shrubs and non-native plants. Elevated levels of CO_2, for example, increase growth of grasses but decrease their quality as a livestock food source. This decrease occurs because higher concentrations of CO_2 both reduce the digestibility of the grasses and cause a decline in the concentration of nitrogen and protein in the plants. Invasive non-native plants—which often have traits that allow them to take advantage of warmer temperatures and higher levels of CO_2—pose another significant threat to the quantity and quality of rangeland grasses. One troublesome invasive species, for example, is cheatgrass (*Bromus tectorum*)—a winter annual grass that originated in Europe and Asia and came to the United States in the 1890s. Cheatgrass is unpalatable to most livestock, so cattle and sheep tend to overgraze on native grasses wherever cheatgrass begins to grow. In addition, cheatgrass has a growing cycle opposite that of most native grasses; it typically matures early in the spring, often sucking up much of the water in the top foot of soil and leaving native grasses with an insufficient water supply during hot summer months. Cheatgrass then dies off in the late summer, providing a volatile fuel source for wildfires that can burn off and kill many native plants. In these ways, cheatgrass can slowly become more and more dominant, reducing the quality of rangelands and resulting in an overall decline in livestock productivity.

levels and changes in rainfall and temperatures will have "significant impacts on grasslands and rangelands, with production increases in humid temperate grasslands, but decreases in arid and semiarid regions."[1] Grasslands typically are found in areas of low rainfall, such as the North American prairies, but some grasslands are also located in regions with higher precipitation levels, such as parts of Europe, of New Zealand, and of North and South America. Rangelands, which include vegetation such as desert plants, scrub, and chaparral, are found in drier regions.

'Warming up to 2°C suggests positive impacts on pasture and livestock productivity in humid temperate regions. By contrast, negative impacts are predicted in arid and semiarid regions.'

Recent studies have shown that climate changes are likely to damage many arid grasslands as traditional grass varieties die off and are overwhelmed by stronger, but less nutritious, plants. One 2003 study, for example, found that elevated CO_2 levels and increased nitrogen in a California grassland composed of annual grass species caused decreased plant diversity in just three years, although diversity did increase with more rainfall (even amid warmer temperatures). In addition, a 2004 study by British climate scientists of 1,350 European plant species predicted that half of these species will become vulnerable or endangered by 2080 because of hotter temperatures and precipitation changes. As the IPCC explains, "Large areas of upland Britain are already colonised by relatively unpalatable plant species such as bracken, matt grass and tor grass. At elevated CO_2 further changes may be expected in the dominance of these species, which could have detrimental effects on the nutritional value of extensive grasslands to grazing animals."[2] Notably, however, in areas that are seeded with legumes (plants that produce peas or beans), studies showed that elevated CO_2 levels increased plant development.

Recent evidence confirms these findings, according to the IPCC. Noting that animals require a level of 7 to 8 percent of crude proteins in their pasture to maintain good health (and up to 24 percent for high-producing dairy cows), the 2007 IPCC report concludes that reductions in crude protein under elevated CO_2 could make pastures in some areas insufficient for grazing animals, but that factors such as the increase in legume production could help compensate for this protein dip in wild pastures.

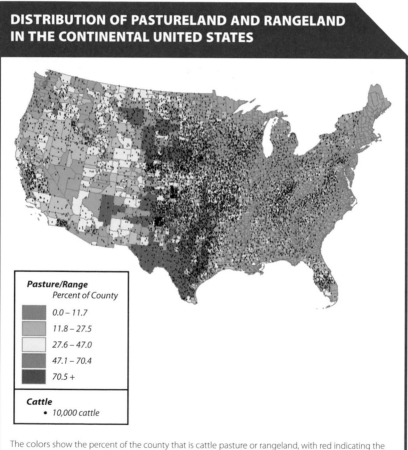

DISTRIBUTION OF PASTURELAND AND RANGELAND IN THE CONTINENTAL UNITED STATES

Pasture/Range
Percent of County

- 0.0 – 11.7
- 11.8 – 27.5
- 27.6 – 47.0
- 47.1 – 70.4
- 70.5 +

Cattle
- 10,000 cattle

The colors show the percent of the county that is cattle pasture or rangeland, with red indicating the highest percentage. Each dot represents 10,000 cattle. Livestock production occurs in every state. Increasing concentration of carbon dioxide reduces the quality of forage, necessitating more acreage and resulting in a decline in livestock productivity.

Source: U.S. Global Change Research Program, "Global Climate Change Impacts in the United States," eds. T.R. Karl, T.M. Melillo, and T.C. Peterson, New York: Cambridge University Press, 2009. www.globalchange.gov.

In addition, data suggest that mild warming generally increases grassland productivity, at least as long as those areas receive sufficient rainfall.

Decreases and greater variability in rainfall are expected to take place in several major grassland and rangeland areas (such as South America, southern and northern Africa, western Asia, Australia, and southern Europe), however, and these impacts could significantly reduce grassland productivity. Overall, the 2007 IPCC report predicts that temperature increases are likely to cause damage to many grassland areas in already dry regions. As the report states, "Warming up to 2°C suggests positive impacts on pasture and livestock productivity in humid temperate regions. By contrast, negative impacts are predicted in arid and semiarid regions."[3]

Finally, the 2007 IPCC report notes that many of the world's rangelands are affected by the El Niño Southern Oscillation, a climate pattern in the tropical Pacific ocean that involves warming or cooling of surface waters and can cause droughts, floods, and other weather disturbances on land areas around the world. The IPCC says these events could intensify with future climate changes, and in dry regions could lead to reduced rainfall, soil degradation, and reduced vegetation growth with a corresponding loss of pasturelands and farmlands.

Heat Stress on Animals

Hotter temperatures caused by climate change can also affect livestock directly, in the form of heat stress. As the 2007 IPCC report puts it, "Thermal stress reduces [animal] productivity [and] conception rates and is potentially life-threatening to livestock."[4] The report explains that studies show higher temperatures can cause declines in eating and grazing, decreases in dairy milk production, and altered conception rates for animals, particularly cattle, whose breeding season typically occurs in spring and summer. The U.S. Global Change Research Program explains this phenomenon further:

Temperature and humidity interact to cause stress in animals, just as in humans; the higher the heat and humidity, the greater the stress and discomfort, and the larger the reduction in the animals' ability to produce milk, gain weight, and reproduce. Milk production declines in dairy operations, the number of days it takes for cows to reach their target weight grows longer in meat operations, conception rate in cattle falls, and swine growth rates decline due to heat. As a result, swine, beef, and milk production are all projected to decline in a warmer world.[5]

Climate changes and weather variations could even kill livestock, according to the IPCC. Unpredictable, extreme weather patterns could pose the highest risk, especially for animals that may not be properly conditioned or provided with help adapting to quickly changing weather. In fact, severe weather events such as heat waves and snowstorms are already affecting animal production in the United States. As J.L. Hatfield of the U.S. Department of Agriculture's Agricultural Research Service explains:

> In the central U.S. in 1992, 1995, 1997, 1999, 2005, and 2006, some feedlots (intensive cattle feeding operations) lost in excess of 100 head each during severe heat episodes. The heat waves of 1995 and 1999 were particularly severe with documented cattle losses in individual states approaching 5,000 head each year. . . . The winter of 1996–[19]97 also caused hardship for cattle producers because of greater than normal snowfall and wind velocity, with some feedlots reporting losses in excess of 1,000 head. During that winter, up to 50 percent of the newborn calves were lost, and more than 100,000 head of cattle died in the Northern Plains of the United States. Additional snowstorm losses were incurred with the collapse of and/ or loss of power to buildings that housed confined domestic livestock. Early snowstorms in 1992 and 1997 resulted in the loss of more than 30,000 head of feedlot cattle each year in the southern plains of the United States.[6]

Studies in Africa and other regions tell a similar tale, showing a strong correlation between drought and animal deaths.

The climate impact on livestock production will probably be felt most strongly in the developing world, where an estimated 1 billion poor people rely on small farms and livestock systems to provide their livelihoods. For these small farmers, raising livestock often lessens the risks of crop farming and provides critical additional income. As the cumulative effects of climate change develop in these regions, many poor farmers are likely to become even poorer. Experts say that animal producers can alleviate some of these climate impacts by developing more heat-tolerant breeds of animals or by helping animals to adapt to climate changes. Appropriate countermeasures for high temperatures, for example, might include providing grazing animals with sunshades or increasing evaporative cooling by setting up water mists combined with fans or other ventilation. These adaptations will create additional costs that may be too high for farmers who are already struggling for economic survival, however.

Impacts on Fisheries

In addition to farmed crops and livestock, fish provide another important global food source. The Food and Agriculture Organization of the United Nations estimates that fish provide more than 2.6 billion people with a minimum of 20 percent of their average per capita animal protein intake. Wild fishing areas account for the majority of fish production, and the rest is produced by fish farming, or aquaculture. According to the IPCC, aquaculture is similar to land animal production in many ways, and it is similarly vulnerable to climate changes. For example, fish can experience stress from increases in temperature and water acidity, and they can be harmed by extreme weather events such as intense storms, hurricanes, and cyclones. Fish farms also depend on the availability of safe and clean water, both freshwater and seawater, as well as on fishmeal food, which is often made from wild fish. On the other hand, aquaculture could benefit from climate change in areas where warmer temperatures decrease the amount of ice, help fish to grow faster, and prolong fish growing seasons.

The 2007 IPCC report provides more specifics about the climate effects on aquaculture. One study cited by the report, for example, showed positive growth effects for rainbow trout with a 3.6°F (2°C) increase in winter temperatures but negative effects with the same temperature increase in summer. According to the IPCC, therefore, "temperature increases may cause seasonal increases in growth, but also risks to fish populations at the upper end of their thermal tolerance zone."[7] Already, the report notes, the effects of rising temperatures can be seen in marine and freshwater ecosystems in areas such as the northeastern Atlantic, where rapid temperature changes have caused fish populations to shift northward, and some local extinctions have begun to occur in certain species. Warmer water temperatures have also encouraged the growth of algae—aquatic plants that grow on surface

Rainbow trout are among the species of fish affected by rapid temperature changes in marine and freshwater ecosystems. © Mark Conline/Alamy.

waters. Algae crowds out other plants that fish use for food, and its decomposition starves fish of oxygen.

Scientists predict that future climate changes will continue to have a significant impact on fisheries (a term that encompasses both wild fishing areas and fish farms), but the global impact is not fully known. The evidence so far, however, is not encouraging. Data from the Pacific and Atlantic oceans, the IPCC says, suggest that the nutrient supply for fish is declining because of changes in ocean currents and in nutrients brought by winds. Although this effect varies by region, some areas have recorded steady declines in wild fish catches since the 1970s. In addition, simulations designed to measure the ocean's response to future climate warming have shown global increases in fish production but significant problems in certain areas. Simulations, for example, show a 50 percent decline of North Atlantic plankton—tiny organisms that form the basis of the ocean's food system, produce half the world's oxygen, and destroy harmful carbon dioxide. A 2010 study published in *Nature* concluded that warming sea-surface temperatures have already caused a 40 percent decline in phytoplankton since 1950. According to the IPCC, this evidence provides "grounds for concern that aquatic production, including fisheries production, will suffer regional and possibly global decline and that this has already begun."[8]

The 2007 IPCC report also warns that climate change could cause a northward spread of pathogens, or germs, that could infect and possibly kill certain species of fish. Warmer temperatures and other climate changes, for example, have been shown to spread two specific parasites from the Gulf of Mexico to the Delaware Bay and other northern locations, where they caused the death of many oysters. Areas likely to suffer the most economic damage from harm to fisheries, according to the IPCC, are central and northern Asian countries, the western Sahel coast in Africa, coastal tropical regions of South America, and some smaller island nations. The bottom line for global fish production, as the U.S. Fish and Wildlife Service puts it on its Web site, is that "some [fish] species will adapt successfully to an abruptly warming world; many will struggle; and others will disappear."[9]

The threat from climate change thus extends to all forms of agriculture—crops, livestock, and fisheries—but the degree of impact varies depending on location.

Notes

1. International Panel on Climate Change (IPCC), "Chapter 5: Food, Fibre and Forest Products," in *Climate Change 2007: Impacts, Adaptation and Vulnerability: Contribution of Working Group II to the Fourth Assessment Report*, eds. M.L. Parry, O.F. Canziani, J.P. Palutikof, P.J. van der Linden, and C.E. Hanson, New York: Cambridge University Press, 2008, p. 285. www.ipcc.ch.
2. IPCC, "Chapter 5: Food, Fibre and Forest Products," p. 287.
3. IPCC, "Chapter 5: Food, Fibre and Forest Products," p. 288.
4. IPCC, "Chapter 5: Food, Fibre and Forest Products," p. 287.
5. U.S. Global Change Research Program, "Global Climate Change Impacts in the United States," New York: Cambridge University Press, 2009, p. 78. www .globalchange.gov.
6. J.L. Hatfield, "The Effects of Climate Change on Livestock Production," *The Pig Site*, June 2008. www.thepigsite.com.
7. IPCC, "Chapter 5: Food, Fibre and Forest Products," p. 291.
8. IPCC, "Chapter 5: Food, Fibre and Forest Products," p. 292.
9. U.S. Fish and Wildlife Service, "Climate Change," May 11, 2010. www.fws.gov.

The Impact of Projected Climate Changes on U.S. and World Agriculture

The negative impacts of climate change on agriculture will be felt differently in different parts of the world. The United Nations Intergovernmental Panel on Climate Change (IPCC) has consistently predicted that developing countries, which mostly are found in low-latitude regions, are likely to suffer more from global warming than developed countries located in higher latitude regions. Africa and Asia, scientists agree, are most at risk; climate changes in these areas could reduce crop yields significantly and require countries to import more and more of their food. Developed regions, such as countries in Europe and North America, will be less affected by coming climate changes, but certain parts of these places will also experience major changes in rainfall and temperatures, and they may be challenged to maintain current agricultural production levels.

Developed Versus Developing Countries

The IPCC's 2007 report confirms its earlier projections, citing studies that suggest potentially large negative climate impacts in low-latitude agriculture (developing countries) but benefits from climate changes in mid latitudes to high latitudes (developed countries). One study, for example, concluded that there will be major gains in potential agricultural land by 2080, particularly in North America (20 to 50 percent) and Russia (40 to

CLIMATE EFFECTS ON CROP YIELDS IN DEVELOPED AND DEVELOPING COUNTRIES

Region	CSIRO no CF	NCAR no CF	CSIRO CF	NCAR CF
Maize, irrigated				
Developing countries	−2.0	−2.8	−1.4	−2.1
Developed countries	−1.2	−8.7	−1.2	−8.6
Maize, rainfed				
Developing countries	0.2	−2.9	2.6	−0.8
Developed countries	0.6	−5.7	9.5	2.5
Rice, irrigated				
Developing countries	−14.4	−18.5	2.4	−0.5
Developed countries	−3.5	−5.5	10.5	9.0
Rice, rainfed				
Developing countries	−1.3	−1.4	6.5	6.4
Developed countries	17.3	10.3	23.4	17.8
Wheat, irrigated				
Developing countries	−28.3	−34.3	−20.8	−27.2
Developed countries	−5.7	−4.9	−1.3	−0.1
Wheat, rainfed				
Developing countries	−1.4	−1.1	9.3	8.5
Developed countries	3.1	2.4	9.7	9.5

For each crop and management system, this table reports the area weighed average change (percent) in yield for a crop grown with 2050 climate instead of 2000 climate. CF = CO_2 fertilization; No CF = without CO_2 fertilization. CSIRO = As predicted by the Australian Commonwealth Scientific and Industrial Research Organization. NCAR = As predicted by the National Center for Atmospheric Research.

Source: International Food Policy Research Institute, "Climate Change, Impact on Agriculture and Costs of Adaptation," October 2009, p. 5. www.ifpri.org.

70 percent), but losses of up to 9 percent in sub-Saharan Africa. Agricultural land is gained when warming temperatures open up regions that were once too cold to support agriculture, and it is lost when hotter temperatures turn arable land—that is, land

suitable for cultivation—into arid desert. Because agricultural production may decrease in lower latitudes, the IPCC predicts that by 2080 grain imports by developing countries could rise by 10 to 40 percent. According to the IPCC, the developing countries likely to face the biggest challenges in agriculture and food security from climate changes are in southern Africa and southern Asia.

The IPCC cautions that these predictions are subject to many variables, however, and that there is still a possibility that developed countries could be surprised by significant negative climate impacts on agricultural production, even before the middle of the twenty-first century. A 2002 study cited by the IPCC, for example, found that the global climate impact on agriculture could vary widely. The study concluded that the impact of climate change by 2080 on global agricultural gross domestic product (GDP)—an economic measure of total agricultural output—could be either negative (-1.5 percent) or positive ($+2.6$ percent), with significant regional variation.

'Agricultural production, including access to food, in many African countries and regions is projected to be severely compromised by climate variability and change.'

Climate Challenges for Africa

Africa will be especially vulnerable to climate change, particularly its agricultural sector. Agriculture is a source of jobs and a major contributor to the economies of many countries in Africa. Farmers in many parts of the continent already have to cope with difficult agricultural conditions, including poor soils, numerous

---

Following page: Climate changes in Niger and other African nations may have devastating effects on farmers already affected by widespread poverty and lack of infrastructure. Karen Kasmauski/Science Faction/Getty Images.

pests and crop diseases, a lack of access to high-quality seeds and fertilizers, and extreme weather challenges such as prolonged droughts and floods. Also, many African countries lack the ability to adapt to climate changes because of developmental challenges like widespread poverty, limited access to capital and technology, and existing environmental degradation.

Future climate changes in Africa—which could include temperature increases up to 16.2°F (9°C), decreases in rainfall, more frequent and prolonged droughts, and an increase in the frequency and severity of tropical storms and cyclones—will only heighten these challenges and in some cases significantly restrict agricultural production. By the 2080s, for example, the IPCC report predicts that Africa will experience a significant decrease in rain-fed land (that is, land that receives enough rainfall to grow crops), and a 5 to 8 percent increase in areas of arid and semiarid land. The IPCC says one result, based on a 2005 study led by climate scientist Gunther Fischer, is that "wheat production is likely to disappear from Africa by the 2080s."[1] The IPCC report concludes:

> Agricultural production, including access to food, in many African countries and regions is projected to be severely compromised by climate variability and change. The area suitable for agriculture, the length of growing seasons and yield potential, particularly along the margins of semi-arid and arid areas, are expected to decrease. This would further adversely affect food security and exacerbate malnutrition [on] the continent. In some countries, yields from rain-fed agriculture could be reduced by up to 50% by 2020.[2]

The 2007 IPCC report indicates that parts of the Sahara—a desert area that stretches across northern Africa—appear to be the most vulnerable to coming climate changes. This region, the IPCC says, may face agricultural losses of between 2 and 7 percent of GDP. By comparison, western and central Africa are expected to see losses of 2 to 4 percent, and in other parts of Africa, the losses may be only in the range of 0.4 to 1.3 percent. A select few areas—such as the Ethiopian highlands and parts of southern Africa—could benefit from climate changes such as longer growing seasons and increased rainfall.

Africa's fish and livestock production will also be threatened by rising water and air temperatures. Various studies cited by the IPCC show, for example, that slight global temperature increases of 2.7°F to 3.6°F (1.5°C to 2.0°C) could harm fisheries in northwest Africa and the East African lakes, and that coastal lagoons and lakes could be affected by an inflow of saltwater because of rising sea levels. In addition, simulations show that extreme weather such as high winds and storms could decrease fish productivity by 50–60 percent. Similarly, according to the IPCC, moderate warming of 4.5°F (2.5°C)—which can cause deterioration of rangelands and animal heat stress—would likely decrease the income of larger livestock farms by 22 percent, and warming of 9°F (5°C) could reduce income by as much as 35 percent.

Climate Effects in Asia

Another part of the world that the IPCC projects will be greatly affected by climate change is Asia. There, melting of glaciers in the Himalayan mountains is projected to initially increase flooding, then to lead to decreased river flows as the glaciers recede. By the 2050s, the IPCC says, there will be less freshwater in central, South, East, and Southeast Asia's river basins—a change that could affect more than a billion people. Coastal regions, especially heavily populated areas, will be threatened by rising seas and, in some cases, rising river deltas. These changes, along with warmer temperatures, decreasing rainfall, and other climate impacts, could significantly alter Asian agricultural production.

The 2007 IPCC report concludes that "crop yields could increase up to 20% in East and South-East Asia while they could decrease up to 30% in central and South Asia by the mid-21st century."[3] More specifically, the IPCC projects about a 2.5 to 10 percent decrease in crop yield for parts of Asia in the 2020s and a 5 to 30 percent decrease in the 2050s. Grain crops such as wheat, corn, and rice are likely to be the most affected. For example, the combination of heat stress and water scarcity, the IPCC estimates, could cause rice production in Asia to decline by 3.8 percent by the end of the twenty-first century. Studies indicate that climate impacts vary by region, however. In Bangladesh, for example, studies show that production of rice might drop by 8 percent by the year 2050, while some areas in central and southern Japan might see decreased rice yields of up to 40 percent. Furthermore, even moderate global temperature increases (3.6°F or 2°C) could reduce rain-fed wheat yield in India by 2 to 5 percent and reduce rain-fed rice yield in China by 5 to 12 percent. With higher temperature increases, rice and wheat yield in South Asia could drop even more.

In addition, the Asia-Pacific region—the world's largest producer of fish, both farmed and wild-caught—faces threats to its fisheries. The IPCC says recent studies suggest that climate changes will cause "a reduction of primary [fish] production in the tropical oceans because of changes in oceanic circulation in a warmer atmosphere,"[4] as phenomena such as warmer temperatures, changes in fish migration routes, and increased El Niño events (a climate pattern in the tropical Pacific Ocean that causes weather disturbances on land) affect the coastal waters of East, South, and Southeast Asia. In northern Asian areas, moderate warming could improve some fisheries but is likely to decrease shrimp production.

Climate Changes in Europe, Latin America, and Australia

More developed parts of the world might not be as seriously affected by climate changes as less developed regions, but virtually no place on the planet will escape negative climate impacts. In Europe, for example, the IPCC predicts:

Nearly all European regions are anticipated to be negatively affected by some future impacts of climate change, and these will pose challenges to many economic sectors. Climate change is expected to magnify regional differences in Europe's natural resources and assets. Negative impacts will include increased risk of inland flash floods, and more frequent coastal flooding and increased erosion (due to storminess and sea-level rise). The great majority of organisms and ecosystems will have difficulty adapting to climate change.[5]

Southern Europe could be the hardest hit, the IPCC says, because climate change will exacerbate already difficult conditions of high temperatures and drought and will reduce water availability and crop production substantially. In central and eastern Europe, summer rainfall is expected to decrease somewhat, and in northern Europe climate change could bring mixed results, with increased crop yields because of warming temperatures and elevated levels of CO_2, but also negative effects over the long term such as more frequent winter floods.

Climate changes will affect Latin America in similar ways, although more severely. Not only are parts of the region's tropical forest expected to be replaced by more arid vegetation, but the IPCC also predicts that drier areas may experience increased salinization and desertification of agricultural land. According to the 2007 IPCC report, the result will be that "productivity of some important crops is projected to decrease and livestock productivity to decline, with adverse consequences for food security."[6]

Meanwhile, already parched countries, such as Australia, will face serious challenges as reduced rainfall, increased evaporation, and more frequent wildfires cause the region to become even less receptive to agriculture. The 2007 IPCC report therefore states that "production from agriculture . . . is projected to decline over much of southern and eastern Australia . . . due to increased drought and fire."[7]

Climate Impacts in the United States and Canada

The United States, like Europe, will be far less affected by climate change than many developing countries, but it too will suffer negative impacts. According to the IPCC's 2007 report, temperatures will be significantly warmer across the whole North American continent during the next century, with temperature increases of 3.6°F to 5.4°F (2°C to 3°C) on the coasts, and significantly higher temperature increases (9°F to 18°F, or 5°C to 10°C) inland, especially over Canada and Alaska. Much of the continent will experience increases in precipitation, except for the U.S. Southwest, which will see an increase in drought conditions. Largely as a result of extra rainfall, the IPCC predicts that overall yields of rain-fed agriculture in the United States will increase by 20 percent in the early decades of the twenty-first century, assuming modest climate change. Yet even with modest warming, the IPCC predicts that crops currently near climate thresholds, such as wine grapes in California, orange crops in the southeastern United States, and corn in the huge midwestern U.S. corn belt, could suffer decreases in quality and yields.

Moreover, rainfall will vary widely among regions, and limited water resources in certain areas will pose additional challenges for some crops. For example, the IPCC projects that warming in the western mountains of North America will cause "decreased snowpack, more winter flooding, and reduced summer flows, exacerbating competition for over-allocated water resources."[8] Loss of snowpack water, combined with reduced precipitation, will mean less water for irrigation at the same time that warmer temperatures will result in increased demand for irrigation water.

California will suffer greatly, according to IPCC projections. Water is essential to this dry region, and the agriculture sector is the biggest consumer of California's water. Scientists say that California will face prolonged hot spells and significant decreases in precipitation and in the Sierra mountain snowpack that pro-

Warmer Temperatures and Maple Syrup Production in Vermont

Warmer temperatures brought by climate change could spell the end of maple syrup production in Vermont—a state historically known for its maple trees and syrup production. Real maple syrup is produced from the sap of maple trees, and the sap flows only when temperatures are exactly right—when night temperatures drop to about 21.2°F (−6°C) and when daytime temperatures rise to about 39.2°F (4°C). Global warming, however, is disrupting traditional schedules for maple syrup production and is pushing the industry northward, toward Canada. Typically, maple trees were tapped beginning in early March, but over the last decade producers have begun tapping earlier and earlier. In addition, the end of the season now comes much earlier. As temperatures warm even more, climate experts say these effects could multiply, decreasing the growing season for maples and reducing syrup production. Some computer models even suggest that Vermont maples could be wiped out completely. The beneficiary of this climate change will probably be Canada's province of Quebec, because warmer temperatures there could provide a longer growing season for maples. Canada has begun to develop this industry; it already produces 80 percent of the world's supply of maple syrup, compared to 20 percent produced by the United States.

vides much of the state's water—climate impacts that could spell disaster for many California crops. As a 2009 report by the U.S. Global Change Research Program explains:

Much of the [Southwest] region's agriculture will experience detrimental impacts in a warmer future, particularly specialty crops in California such as apricots, almonds, artichokes, figs, kiwis, olives, and walnuts. These and other specialty crops require a minimum number of hours at a chilling temperature threshold in the winter to become dormant and set fruit for the following year. . . . A steady reduction in winter chilling could have serious economic impacts on fruit and nut production in the region. California's losses due to future climate change are estimated between zero and 40 percent for wine and table grapes, almonds, oranges, walnuts, and avocadoes, varying significantly by location.[9]

In fact, according to a May 2007 study published in the journal *Science*, within just a few years or decades, the U.S. Southwest could suffer heat and drought comparable to that of the 1930s Dust Bowl in the Midwest. Such conditions could destroy California's vibrant $30 billion per year agriculture economy in the state's rich Central Valley, which now produces more than a quarter of the nation's fruits, nuts, and vegetables. As U.S. Secretary of Energy Steven Chu has suggested, "We're looking at a scenario where there's no more agriculture in California."[10]

U.S. livestock and fisheries will also be negatively affected. Studies predict, for example, that confined pig, beef, and dairy milk production in the United States could decline as much as 2.2 percent by 2050 because of climate changes. Also, according to the 2007 IPCC report, "Cold-water fisheries [in the United States] will likely be negatively affected by climate change."[11] Arctic freshwater fishing areas will be the most affected, because they will experience the steepest temperature increases. U.S. warm-water fisheries may benefit from climate change with greater yield, and cool-water fisheries will face mixed impacts.

The United States thus will undergo its share of farming challenges because of climate change—challenges that could lead to food production declines.

Notes

1. Intergovernmental Panel on Climate Change (IPCC), "Chapter 9: Africa," in *Climate Change 2007: Impacts, Adaptation and Vulnerability: Contribution of Working Group*

II to the Fourth Assessment Report, edited by M.L. Parry, O.F. Canziani, J.P. Palutikof, P.J. van der Linden, and C.E. Hanson, New York: Cambridge University Press, 2008, p. 448.

2. IPCC, "Technical Summary," in *Climate Change 2007: Impacts, Adaptation and Vulnerability,* p. 48.
3. IPCC, "Technical Summary," p. 59.
4. IPCC, "Chapter 10: Asia," in *Climate Change 2007: Impacts, Adaptation and Vulnerability*, p. 482.
5. IPCC, "Summary for Policymakers," in *Climate Change 2007: Impacts, Adaptation and Vulnerability*, p. 14.
6. IPCC, "Summary for Policymakers," p. 14.
7. IPCC, "Summary for Policymakers," p. 14.
8. IPCC, "Summary for Policymakers," p. 14.
9. U.S. Global Change Research Program, *Global Climate Change Impacts in the United States*, edited by Thomas R. Karl, Jerry M. Melillo, and Thomas C. Peterson, New York: Cambridge University Press, 2009, p. 134. www.globalchange.gov.
10. Quoted in Jim Tankersley, "California Farms, Vineyards in Peril from Warming, U.S. Energy Secretary Warns," *Los Angeles Times*, February 4, 2009. www.latimes.com.
11. IPCC, "Chapter 14: North America," in *Climate Change 2007: Impacts, Adaptation and Vulnerability*, p. 631.

CHAPTER 6

Global Warming and Food Security

Scientists warn that the negative impacts of climate change on crops, livestock, and fisheries could ultimately decrease global food production and threaten food security in many regions. As the United Nations Intergovernmental Panel on Climate Change (IPCC) states in its 2007 report, "All four dimensions of food security, namely food availability (i.e., production and trade), stability of food supplies, access to food, and food utilisation will likely be affected by climate change."[1] Scientists say that climate impacts on food production will vary from region to region, however, with many developing countries—which, with limited land and water resources, may already face challenges producing enough food—experiencing the brunt of negative impacts. Southern Africa, for example, could become the most food-insecure region in the world because of severe drought conditions. At the same time, food security will also be affected by a number of non-climate-related factors, such as poverty, population growth, economics, trade issues, and rising food production costs.

Defining Food Security

According to the Food and Agriculture Organization of the United Nations (FAO), food security has four components—food availability, food accessibility, food utilization, and food system stability. Food availability refers to the process of producing and distributing crops and other foods, and it can be affected by climate changes that cause water or land scarcities as well as by non-climate factors such as rising fuel prices. For example, if crop yields decrease, or the cost of producing food increases, there may be less food available in global or local food markets.

Food accessibility concerns whether people have the resources and ability to obtain available food supplies. If food prices increase in coming years because of the pressure of climate change on agriculture, poor people may not be able to afford enough food for a healthy diet, making them vulnerable to hunger and malnutrition. Their ability to obtain food may depend on the existence of governmental or international food aid. Other issues that could affect accessibility include whether nations with insufficient food can procure enough food through global trade systems and whether they can distribute this food to the locations where it is most needed.

Food utilization encompasses such concepts as food nutrition, food preparation and storage, and food safety—that is, whether the available and accessible food is able to provide the nutrients needed by people in a safe and reliable way. People might have an abundance of staple foods yet still be vulnerable to malnutrition if these foods lack the variety necessary to satisfy nutritional requirements. Climate changes could cause malnutrition if rising food prices limit people's ability to purchase a diversity of foods. Climate changes could also affect the nutritional value in some foods either positively or negatively; for example, in some areas higher levels of CO_2 could enhance growth and nutrition, while in other areas higher temperatures and reduced precipitation could create drought conditions that have the opposite effect. Food safety could also become an important issue as the climate warms, because wetter or drier conditions could affect food storage and processing options, and warmer temperatures could increase the transmission of foodborne and waterborne diseases.

Food system stability is determined by whether global and local food processing, storage, and marketing systems can continue to operate efficiently in the face of challenges such as climate variability and food emergencies. Climate change could create difficulties for the transportation and distribution of food to some regions following weather-related disasters, for example. Changing climates could also affect crop cycles, cause sudden crop losses, and generally make it difficult to maintain stable food production.

Climate Impacts on Global Food Supplies

Climate Change 2001, the IPCC's Third Assessment Report, predicted that the impact of global warming on global food systems might be relatively minor in the first half of the twenty-first century but progressively negative after that period. The 2001 report also predicted that developing countries will be most at risk for food insecurity, whereas developed regions in some cases may benefit from positive climate change impacts, such as longer growing seasons and higher levels of CO_2. These predictions have been confirmed in numerous studies in recent years.

Because climate change is expected to cause comparatively limited damage to agriculture in developed regions that today produce much of the world's food supply, some studies have predicted that the global impact on world food production may be relatively small. Other studies, however, project significant negative climate impacts in key food-producing regions of developed countries as early as mid-century, so the IPCC cautions that the true impact of climate changes on the world's food supply is as yet uncertain.

Various climate factors could affect future food production, including, for example, just how much average global temperatures rise in coming decades. Moderate warming could increase food production, whereas higher temperatures could harm productivity. As the 2007 IPCC report states, "Globally, the potential for food production is projected to increase with increases in local average temperature over a range of 1 to 3°C, but above this it is projected to decrease."[2] The severity of other aspects of climate change, such as extreme storms, droughts and flooding, and loss of cultivated land, will also affect the stability of food supplies, according to the IPCC. And food prices will be affected by food productivity declines, with prices likely to rise if temperatures reach high ranges.

The IPCC's overall conclusion . . . is that 'climate change is likely to increase the number of people at risk of hunger.'

Various studies have sought to assess the impacts of climate change on food security. According to a 2007 study by researchers at the Carnegie Institution and Lawrence Livermore National Laboratory, for example, warming temperatures over the last two decades have already led to a fall in the yield of some of the world's most important food crops. The study compared yields for the world's six main staple crops—wheat, rice, corn, soybeans, barley, and sorghum—and found that between 1981 and 2002, warmer temperatures caused a loss in production of wheat, corn, and barley of approximately 40 million tons a year and annual losses of roughly $5 billion for major food crops. Climate scientists Christopher Field and David Lobell found that global yields for several of the crops decreased in warmer temperatures, with yields dropping by about 3–5 percent for every 1°F (.55°C) increase. As Field and Lobell write, "Though the [climate] impacts are relatively small compared to the technological [crop] yield gains over the same period, the results demonstrate that negative impacts are already occurring."[3] Other researchers have projected additional negative impacts in the future. Scientist Gunther Fischer and his colleagues, for example, project that climate change will increase the number of undernourished people in 2080 by 5–26 percent, or between 5 million and 170 million people.[4]

EFFECTS OF CLIMATE CHANGE ON FOOD SECURITY

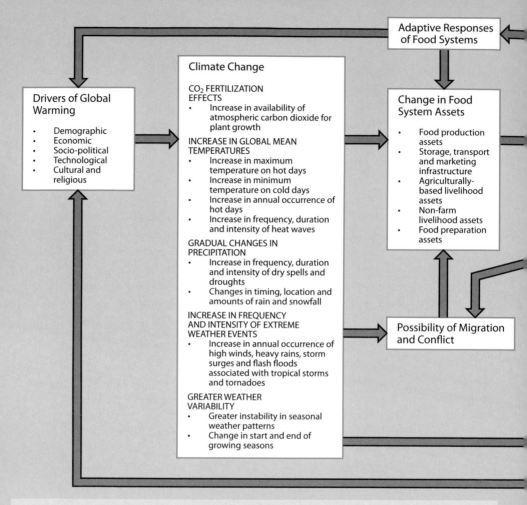

Drivers of Global Warming

- Demographic
- Economic
- Socio-political
- Technological
- Cultural and religious

Climate Change

CO₂ FERTILIZATION EFFECTS
- Increase in availability of atmospheric carbon dioxide for plant growth

INCREASE IN GLOBAL MEAN TEMPERATURES
- Increase in maximum temperature on hot days
- Increase in minimum temperature on cold days
- Increase in annual occurrence of hot days
- Increase in frequency, duration and intensity of heat waves

GRADUAL CHANGES IN PRECIPITATION
- Increase in frequency, duration and intensity of dry spells and droughts
- Changes in timing, location and amounts of rain and snowfall

INCREASE IN FREQUENCY AND INTENSITY OF EXTREME WEATHER EVENTS
- Increase in annual occurrence of high winds, heavy rains, storm surges and flash floods associated with tropical storms and tornadoes

GREATER WEATHER VARIABILITY
- Greater instability in seasonal weather patterns
- Change in start and end of growing seasons

Adaptive Responses of Food Systems

Change in Food System Assets

- Food production assets
- Storage, transport and marketing infrastructure
- Agriculturally-based livelihood assets
- Non-farm livelihood assets
- Food preparation assets

Possibility of Migration and Conflict

Source: Food and Agriculture Organization of the United Nations, "Climate Change and Food Security: A Framework Document," 2008, p. 13. www.fao.org.

The IPCC's overall conclusion from an analysis of these and other studies is that "climate change is likely to increase the number of people at risk of hunger."[5] Yet the IPCC notes that important questions remain unanswered. For example, there

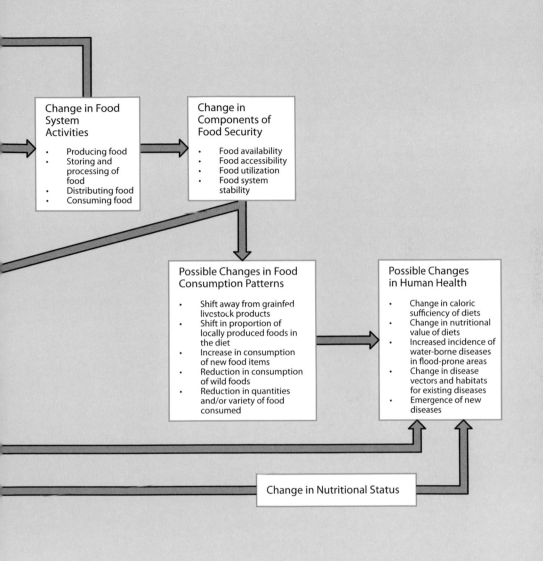

Change in Food System Activities
- Producing food
- Storing and processing of food
- Distributing food
- Consuming food

Change in Components of Food Security
- Food availability
- Food accessibility
- Food utilization
- Food system stability

Possible Changes in Food Consumption Patterns
- Shift away from grainfed livestock products
- Shift in proportion of locally produced foods in the diet
- Increase in consumption of new food items
- Reduction in consumption of wild foods
- Reduction in quantities and/or variety of food consumed

Possible Changes in Human Health
- Change in caloric sufficiency of diets
- Change in nutritional value of diets
- Increased incidence of water-borne diseases in flood-prone areas
- Change in disease vectors and habitats for existing diseases
- Emergence of new diseases

Change in Nutritional Status

is uncertainty about the effects of elevated CO_2 on crops and food security. Most studies suggest that the fertilization effect of CO_2 under various climate change scenarios will not greatly affect global projections of hunger, but under one scenario—that of no CO_2 fertilization—more people will be undernourished in 2080.

Non-Climate Factors Affecting Food Security

The IPCC says that worldwide food security will also depend greatly on non-climate-related socioeconomic developments, such as population increases and economic growth. For example, some studies predict that rapid global economic growth combined with slowing population growth will significantly reduce the number of people at risk of hunger by 2080. Alternatively, if populations continue to grow, economies do not achieve expected growth levels, and poverty levels increase, the number of hungry people rises over coming decades.

Several other factors also are believed to affect food availability and accessibility. Rising energy prices and an uncertain energy future, for example, could have a significant impact since the food system is heavily dependent on fossil fuels for production, processing, distribution, and transportation of food to markets. Similarly, the recent growth of the biofuel industry and the diversion of certain grain crops to biofuels has already made these grains less available for human consumption. As scientist and professor Kenneth G. Cassman wrote in a 2007 article in the online journal *Environmental Research Letters*:

> There is a new urgency to improve the accuracy of predicting climate change impact on crop yields because the balance between food supply and demand is shifting abruptly from surplus to deficit. This reversal is being driven by a rapid rise in petroleum prices and, in response, a massive global expansion of biofuel production from maize, oilseed, and sugar crops. Soon the price of these commodities will be determined by their value as feedstock for biofuel rather than their impor-

---

Following page: Families in isolated, drought-stricken areas of Afghanistan have had to flee their communities in search of food aid. AP Images/Musadeq Sadeq.

tance as human food or livestock feed. The expectation that petroleum prices will remain high and supportive government policies in several major crop producing countries are providing strong momentum for continued expansion of biofuel production capacity and the associated pressures on global food supply.[6]

Cassman explains that these factors could lead to significantly higher prices for food staples for the urban and rural poor in food-importing countries and lower availability of grain for humanitarian aid efforts. In fact, according to the FAO, global food prices (especially prices of grains) spiked by 9 percent in 2006 and 37 percent in 2007—a phenomenon that suggested future food prices could be both inflated and volatile.

At the same time, increasing global demand for meat means that more and more grain crops are being dedicated to animal feed, once again leaving less for human consumption. As vegetarian advocate and writer Stephen Leckie explained in a 2000 article for the International Development Research Centre, a Canadian organization:

> Essentially, the world is experiencing an overpopulation in farm animals. Between 1950 and 1994, global meat production increased nearly fourfold, rising faster than the human population. . . . The combined weight of the world's 15 billion farm animals now surpasses that of the human population by more than a factor of 1.5. In many countries, the affluent are eating the most meat, often at the expense of poorer people who depend on grain supplies increasingly diverted to feed livestock. In China, grain consumption by livestock has increased by a factor of five since 1978. . . . The many farm animals are straining resources and causing environmental harm as a result of their voracious appetites for feed crops and grazing.[7]

Leckie proposes that scaling back on meat production may be the best way to ensure food security in the twenty-first century.

Populations Most at Risk

Many studies reviewed by the IPCC predict that sub-Saharan Africa will become the world's most food-insecure region. Several studies, in fact, project that by 2080 sub-Saharan Africa may account for 40–50 percent of all undernourished people, compared with about 24 percent today. Other estimates are even higher, predicting that the region will be home to 70–75 percent of the world's hungry people, if economic growth is slower than expected.

According to some researchers, however, Africa's food vulnerability is related more to socioeconomic factors than to climate change. Africans, for example, struggle not only with difficult weather but also with such stresses as rampant HIV/AIDS, conflicts over land, and poverty and slow economic growth in some regions. As the climate warms, countries around the world will experience more weather-related disasters, and experts say that these increased disaster risks in Africa will seriously hamper future economic development. Yet climate scientists still do not fully understand, and cannot confidently predict, exactly how much climate change and variability will exacerbate Africa's multiple socioeconomic challenges.

There are concerns about future hunger and malnutrition in Asia, too. Recent studies confirm that climate change will probably adversely affect grasslands, livestock, and water resources in parts of central and Southeast Asia, and that food supplies are likely to be further threatened by the loss of cultivated land and fishery areas in areas along Asia's tropical coasts. The IPCC cautions that the true impact of climate change in Asia is uncertain because of several factors, however. Some Asian countries are already dependent upon other countries for food, and these needier countries may find their supply more sharply reduced than has been predicted. Food supply is also related to customer income and food prices. According to the 2007 IPCC report, "global cereal prices have been projected to increase more than three-fold by the 2080s as a consequence of decline in net pro-

Climate Change and Food Riots

If global or local food production is seriously affected by future climate changes, commentators are predicting that hunger and the threat of starvation in some poor countries may cause food riots, civil unrest, or possibly even massive migration of people from hard-hit areas to places that are less affected by climate impacts. A world food crisis in 2007–2008 provided an example of the type of social instability that can result from food shortages and price increases. During this period, corn prices doubled; wheat prices rose by 50 percent; and rice prices increased by as much as 70 percent in some places. In fact, according to *The Economist* magazine, by the end of 2007 overall food prices had risen 75 percent since 2005, and world grain reserves had dropped to their lowest point ever. Food riots occurred in such places as Haiti, Bangladesh, and Egypt.

Several factors contributed to this recent food crisis, according to economists and other experts. First, governments around the world, including the United States, began diverting corn crops to the production of ethanol—a biofuel that supporters claim can replace gasoline and produce fewer of the carbon emissions that cause global warming. As more land was used for corn production to make ethanol, less wheat was grown, causing an increase in wheat prices. Second, a spike in oil prices caused increases in the cost of fertilizers and transportation used in agriculture, further inflating food prices. Some reports also cited growing demand for more and higher quality food from new middle classes in rapidly developing nations such as India and China, as well as growing pressure on croplands from extreme weather such as floods, drought, and heat waves. As climate change intensifies and many non-climate factors also continue to affect agriculture, many experts predict that the future will bring more social and political instability.

ductivity due to projected climate change."[8] These higher prices could leave greater numbers of poorer people unable to afford a sufficient supply of food. The IPCC therefore concludes that the risk of hunger is likely to remain very high in many Asian countries.

Food Security and the Global Economy

All of the IPCC's predictions about climate change and food security assume that the world food system will continue to function and that the world economy will continue to grow, although such growth may occur at different rates and with significant regional variations. According to the FAO, however, it is also possible that climate change could curtail global economic growth—a development that could jeopardize food security even in developed regions. As the FAO explains,

> If global financial markets are not able to keep pace with continued high losses from extreme weather events, and large numbers of individual households in developed and emerging developing countries experience uncompensated declines in the value of their personal assets and income-generating capacity, global economic recession and a deterioration in the food security situation at all levels is also a possibility, putting everybody at risk.[9]

For this reason, climate scientists and other scholars assert that it is in every nation's interest to try to minimize climate changes and work to maintain a vibrant world agriculture system.

Notes

1. Intergovernmental Panel on Climate Change (IPCC), "Chapter 5: Food, Fibre and Forest Products," in *Climate Change 2007: Impacts, Adaptation and Vulnerability: Contribution of Working Group II to the Fourth Assessment Report*, edited by M.L. Parry, O.F. Canziani, J.P. Palutikof, P.J. van der Linden, and C.E. Hanson, New York: Cambridge University Press, 2008, p. 297. www.ipcc.ch.
2. IPCC, "Chapter 5: Food, Fibre and Forest Products," p. 298.
3. David B. Lobell and Christopher B. Field, "Global Scale Climate-Crop Yield Relationships and the Impacts of Recent Warming," *Environmental Research Letters*, March, 2007. http://iopscience.iop.org.
4. IPCC, "Chapter 5: Food, Fibre and Forest Products," p. 298.

5. IPCC, "Chapter 5: Food, Fibre and Forest Products," p. 298.
6. Kenneth G. Cassman, "Climate Change, Biofuels, and Global Food Security," *Environmental Research Letters*, March 2007. http://iopscience.iop.org.
7. Stephen Leckie, "How Meat-Centred Eating Patterns Affect Food Security and the Environment," International Development Research Centre, 2000. www.idrc.ca.
8. IPCC, "Chapter 10: Asia," in *Climate Change 2007: Impacts, Adaptation and Vulnerability*, p. 482.
9. Food and Agriculture Organization of the United Nations, "Climate Change and Food Security: A Framework Document," 2008, p. 29. www.fao.org.

CHAPTER 7

Farming's Impact on Global Warming

Climate change affects agriculture, but at the same time, agriculture itself is the source of many of the greenhouse gases that scientists believe are causing the climate to warm. According to the United Nations Intergovernmental Panel on Climate Change (IPCC), the three main causes of the increase in greenhouse gases in the earth's atmosphere during the last 250 years are the burning of fossil fuels, land use (including deforestation), and agriculture (including both crop and livestock production). The IPCC's 2007 report estimates that "agriculture accounted for . . . 10–12% of total global anthropogenic [human-caused] emissions of greenhouse gases"[1] in the year 2005. More recent reports say the percentage is much higher. A 2010 report from the International Panel for Sustainable Resource Management, part of the United Nation's Environment Programme, estimated that agriculture accounts for 14 percent of the world's greenhouse gas emissions, and several other reports maintain that the livestock sector alone produces huge amounts of greenhouse gases.

Various farming practices are the root of these harmful emissions. The widespread use of chemical fertilizers on farms produces nitrous oxide (N_2O) and intensive livestock production releases massive amounts of methane (CH_4)—both greenhouse gases even more powerful than carbon dioxide (CO_2). The IPCC estimates that agriculture accounts for about 60 percent of global nitrous oxide emissions and about 50 percent of methane emis-

79 |

sions. Also, farming contributes to global warming indirectly—both because it leads to deforestation (cutting down of carbon-reducing forests) and because large amounts of fossil fuels are required to produce and transport food. Many of these agricultural emissions, according to climate activists, are the result of the industrial farming techniques and global trading systems employed in modern agriculture.

Soil Management and Nitrous Oxide Emissions

One of the potent greenhouse gases produced by agriculture is nitrous oxide (N_2O)—a gas that is about three hundred times more powerful than carbon dioxide in creating climate warming. According to the U.S. Environmental Protection Agency (EPA), for example, nitrous oxide accounts for about 60 percent of total agriculture-produced emissions in the United States. Nitrous oxide is produced naturally in soils through ordinary microbial processes, but these natural emissions are greatly increased by many agricultural practices used today—such as the use of synthetic and organic fertilizers, production of nitrogen-fixing crops, cultivation of high organic content soils, and the application of livestock manure to croplands and pasture. These activities add extra nitrogen to the soil, which increases nitrous oxide emissions.

Although organic fertilizers and manure do add nitrogen to soils, many agricultural experts say that the majority of agricultural nitrous oxide emissions are the result of the synthetic nitrogen fertilizers used in great quantities by industrial farms. Large agricultural corporations in the U.S. Midwest, for example, produce vast amounts of corn—a crop that requires large amounts of nitrogen—by dousing corn crops with chemical fertilizers. This practice is responsible for increasing nitrous oxide emissions as well as nitrogen contamination of waterways and groundwaters. As the environmental group Greenpeace explained in a 2008 report:

One of the biggest problems in industrialised agriculture is the massive overuse of [nitrogen] fertilisers. More than 50 percent of all fertiliser applied to the soil ends up in the atmosphere or in local waterways. One of the most potent greenhouse gases is nitrous oxide (N_2O), with a global warming potential . . . some 296 times higher than that of carbon dioxide. The overuse of

GREENHOUSE GAS EMISSIONS FROM AGRICULTURE

	Annual Emissions [million tons carbon dioxide (CO_2) equivalent]	Greenhouse Gas
Deforestation for agriculture	5,900	
Soil fertilization	2,100	Nitrous oxide (N_2O)
Gases from food digestion in cattle	1,800	Methane (CH_4)
Biomass burning	700	CH_4, N_2O
Paddy (flooded) rice production	600	CH_4
Livestock manure	400	CH_4, N_2O
Other (e.g, delivery of irrigation water)	900	CO_2, N_2O
TOTAL	12,400	

The greenhouse gas impact of nitrous oxide is equivalent to 298 units of carbon dioxide; 1 unit of methane is equivalent to 25 units of carbon dioxide.

Source: Sara J. Scherr and Sajal Sthapit, *Mitigating Climate Change Through Food and Land Use*, Washington, DC: Worldwatch Institute, 2009, p.10.

fertilisers and the resulting nitrous oxide emissions have the highest share of agriculture's contribution to climate change: the equivalent of 2.1 billion tonnes of CO_2 every year. And, the energy-intensive production of fertiliser adds another 410 million tonnes of CO_2-equivalents. Of all chemical products, fertilisers are among the greatest contributors to global greenhouse gas emissions.[2]

Critics say other modern agricultural practices—such as frequent tilling that can destroy arable land, the overuse and waste of groundwater, and monoculture (single crop) techniques that result in biodiversity loss—create more environmental stress and decrease the ability of land and crops to cope with climate changes.

Greenhouse Gases from Livestock Production

According to climate experts, a second big greenhouse gas emitter in agriculture is livestock production, which occupies 70 percent of all agricultural land, or about 30 percent of the land surface of the entire planet. These livestock operations produce large amounts of methane, a greenhouse gas twenty-five times as potent as carbon dioxide. Animal production also produces other types of greenhouse gases—nitrous oxide (from the growing of animal feed with nitrogen fertilizers and the storage and treatment of animal manure) and carbon dioxide (from the use of fossil fuels and deforestation).

'Livestock's contribution . . . currently amounts to about 18 percent of the global warming effect—an even larger contribution than the transportation sector worldwide.'

In fact, according to a 2006 report by the United Nations Food and Agriculture Organization (FAO), livestock are responsible for a significant amount of the total global greenhouse gas

Rice Farming and Global Warming

Although livestock produces the bulk of the methane coming from the agricultural sector, rice farming also puts out a great deal of methane, one of the more potent greenhouse gases.

Rice fields (called paddies) cover much of Asia, and rice production has increased along with Asian and world populations over many decades. According to a 2007 report from the United Nations Intergovernmental Panel on Climate Change (IPCC), rice production was a major cause of rapidly rising methane emissions throughout the twentieth century. In fact, some climate experts estimate that rice farming might be responsible for as much as 10 percent of global methane emissions.

Rice growing produces methane because bacteria thrive in flooded rice paddies. In this oxygen-free environment, the bacteria devour and help to decompose manure used as fertilizer and other organic matter, and the decomposition process releases methane. Scientists say that changes in rice farming techniques, such as using less water and less fertilizer or draining rice fields once or several times during the growing season, could reduce the levels of methane produced. These changes could also decrease rice yields, however—an outcome that might be hard to accept for rice farmers, many of whom operate small fields.

emissions that are believed to be causing climate warming. As the FAO report explains:

Livestock's contribution [to global warming] is enormous. It currently amounts to about 18 percent of the global warming effect—an even larger contribution than the transportation sector worldwide. Livestock contribute about 9 percent of total carbon dioxide emissions, but 37 percent of methane and 65 percent of nitrous oxide.[3]

The independent research group Worldwatch Institute has disputed these FAO findings, however, and attributed an even higher percentage of global greenhouese gases to livestock production. A 2009 report from the group argued that "livestock and their byproducts actually account for . . . 51 percent of annual worldwide GHG [greenhouse gases] emissions."[4] Worldwatch Institute found that the FAO had underestimated certain livestock emissions, including CO_2 emissions from livestock respiration, methane emissions, and emissions from clearing land to graze livestock and grow feed.

Livestock produce methane as a by-product of their normal digestive processes, when microbes in the animals' digestive systems break down fodder in a process called enteric fermentation. Basically, this means that the methane is produced by cows belching and otherwise releasing gas from their stomachs and intestines. Methane is also produced from the decomposition of animal wastes. The use of solid manure as a fertilizer on grasslands or crops is not a major emissions problem, because it decomposes aerobically (that is, using oxygen). The disposal of manure by giant confined-animal facilities is a different story, however; the widespread practice by these facilities of storing manure as a liquid or slurry in lagoons, ponds, tanks, or pits causes anaerobic (without oxygen) decomposition that creates significant methane emissions.

Ruminant animals—mainly beef and dairy cattle—raised and processed in large numbers by corporate producers are the major emitters of methane. As the EPA explains, "An adult cow may be a very small source by itself . . . but with about 100 million cattle in the U.S. and 1.2 billion large ruminants in the world, ruminants are one of the largest methane sources. In the U.S., cattle emit about 5.5 million metric tons of methane per year into the atmosphere, accounting for 20% of U.S. methane emissions."[5] Globally, according to the EPA, ruminant livestock produce about 80 million metric tons (88.18 tons) of methane annually, or about 28 percent of global human-produced methane emissions.

Economic expansion in developing countries such as China and India is changing food preferences and causing a growing demand for meat that is likely to increase emissions from the livestock sector of agriculture. As the FAO's 2006 report explains, "Livestock's impact on the environment . . . is growing and rapidly changing. Global demand for meat, milk, and eggs is fast increasing, driven by rising incomes, growing populations, and urbanization."[6] Meat consumption in China, for example, rose by 42 percent from 1995 to 2003, according to recent expert estimates. This figure is double the average Asian rate of meat consumption and just less than half that of the United States. Experts fear that this growing taste for meat will only continue to skyrocket in the future, putting additional pressure on the environment and contributing to further climate warming.

Deforestation

Agriculture also contributes to climate change because it causes deforestation—the cutting down of forests to create agricultural land for growing crops or grazing animals. Globally, forests cover almost 30 percent of the earth's land areas and act as "carbon sinks" that remove carbon from the atmosphere. Deforestation is a major contributor of greenhouse gas emissions because it removes carbon-reducing trees and plants, eliminating these critical carbon sinks. Often, land clearing methods such as slash and burn, which involves burning much of the timber and brush that is cut down, make matters even worse by releasing additional carbon dioxide into the atmosphere. If the timber and brush are left to decay slowly, this also produces CO_2 emissions, but over a longer period of time.

Climate experts say that the conversion of forest to agricultural land is the single largest source of emissions from changes in land use. According to the 2007 IPCC report, for example, deforestation is responsible for 17.3 percent of global human-caused greenhouse gas emissions each year. The 2007 IPCC report also states that reducing or preventing deforestation would

A farmer in Brazil clears land using a highly damaging slash and burn method that leaves large areas of land deforested. Stephen Ferry/Getty Images.

provide the largest and most immediate carbon reduction impact of all possible mitigation actions.

Deforestation in developed countries such as the United States peaked many decades ago, but today the practice continues at a rapid pace in some of the world's last remaining tropical rainforests, most of which are located in developing countries. As Peter Frumhoff, director of science and policy at the Union of Concerned Scientists, explains, "For many developing countries, deforestation is their largest source of emissions."[7] In fact, according to some analyses, tropical deforestation alone produces 1.5 billion metric tons of carbon annually, or about 20 percent of the total synthetic greenhouse gases released into the atmosphere each year. A key factor in this tropical deforestation is expansion of grazing land for livestock, especially in Latin America. The FAO estimates that about 70 percent of once-forested land in the Amazon basin is now used as pasture, with animal feed crops taking up much of the rest. These grazing lands are being further degraded by overgrazing, compaction, and erosion from livestock activity.

Agriculture's Dependence on Fossil Fuels

Agriculture is also heavily dependent on fossil fuels. In fact, almost every part of the modern, commercial food system uses energy—including the manufacture of fertilizers and pesticides; the running of tractors, combines, and other farm equipment that plant and harvest crops; the storing, refrigeration, processing, and packaging of food products; and the transporting of those products to markets around the world. As British writer Norman Church explains:

> Vast amounts of oil and gas are used as raw materials and energy in the manufacture of fertilisers and pesticides, and as cheap and readily available energy at all stages of food production: from planting, irrigation, feeding and harvesting, through to processing, distribution and packaging. In addition, fossil fuels are essential in the construction and the repair of equipment and infrastructure needed to facilitate this industry, including farm machinery, processing facilities, storage, ships, trucks and roads. The industrial food supply system is one of the biggest consumers of fossil fuels and one of the greatest producers of greenhouse gases. . . . The modern, commercial agricultural miracle that feeds all of us, and much of the rest of the world, is completely dependent on the flow, processing and distribution of oil.[8]

Processed and packaged foods are particularly energy intensive. Researchers at the Swedish Institute for Food and Biotechnology, for example, studied the energy inputs required to produce a particular brand of tomato ketchup. The study found that the entire system of growing the tomatoes and converting them to tomato paste in Italy, and shipping the paste to Sweden, where it was processed and packaged into ketchup, involved more than fifty-two different transport and process stages. It is likely that other ingredients used to make the tomato paste and ketchup, such as sugar, vinegar, spices, and salt, would also have

used energy for production and transport. In addition, marketing the ketchup required the production, transport, and use of
packaging bags from the Netherlands as well as ketchup bottles
made from materials obtained from Japan, Italy, Belgium, the
United States, and Denmark. Finally, cardboard and shrink plas-
tic were used to ship the final product to various markets, where
it was distributed to supermarkets and purchased by consumers
who carried the ketchup home in their gas-powered cars.

Supporters of organic agriculture say that organic farming
is more energy efficient than industrial farming, largely because
it uses fewer synthetically produced fertilizers and pesticides to
grow crops. In addition, organic livestock production typically
relies on grass feed rather than energy-intensive grains. The
organic industry has followed the same system of global trading that is responsible for much of the energy consumption of
conventionally produced food, however. Organic foods, just
like non-organic products, are now transported long distances
around the globe by jets, trains, and trucks—all forms of transportation that create large amounts of CO_2 emissions. A 2007
study by researchers at the University of Alberta in Canada, for
example, found that the environmental costs of "food miles"—
the distance that food is transported from where it is grown or
produced to the grocery store—was the same for both organic
and conventionally grown foods. The researchers recommended
that shoppers try to buy locally produced foods and that government policies consider the CO_2 emissions associated with food
transport.

The agriculture sector of the world economy, therefore, like
many other economic sectors, is reliant on fossil fuels and responsible for a significant portion of global CO_2 emissions, as
well as other types of greenhouse gases. Experts say these gases
can be stabilized and reduced only by changing the ways food is
produced, processed, and distributed.

Notes

1. Intergovernmental Panel on Climate Change (IPCC), "Chapter 8: Agriculture," in *Climate Change 2007: Mitigation: Contribution of Working Group III to the Fourth Assessment Report*, edited by B. Metz, O.R. Davidson, P.R. Bosch, R. Dave, and L.A. Meyer, New York: Cambridge University Press, 2007, p. 499. www.ipcc.ch.
2. Greenpeace, "Cool Farming: Climate Impacts of Agriculture and Mitigation Potential, Summary of Report," January 2008. www.greenpeace.org.
3. Food and Agriculture Organization of the United Nations, "Livestock's Long Shadow: Environmental Issues and Options," 2006, p. 272. www.fao.org.
4. Robert Goodland and Jeff Anhang, "Livestock and Climate Change," Worldwatch Institute, 2009, p. 11. www.worldwatch.org.
5. U.S. Environmental Protection Agency, "Climate Change: Methane: Ruminant Livestock," March 21, 2007. www.epa.gov.
6. Food and Agriculture Organization of the United Nations, "Livestock's Long Shadow: Environmental Issues and Options", 2006, p. 3. www.fao.org.
7. Quoted in Union of Concerned Scientists, "Reducing Tropical Deforestation Is Feasible, Affordable, and Essential to Avoid Dangerous Global Warming, Top Experts Say," May 10, 2007. www.ucsusa.org.
8. Norman Church, "Why Our Food Is So Dependent on Oil," *Energy Bulletin*, April 1, 2005. www.energybulletin.net.

CHAPTER 8

Mitigation and Adaptation in the Agricultural Sector

Because agriculture produces greenhouse gas emissions that contribute to climate change and is in turn affected by those climate changes, it will be critical for farmers to take actions both to mitigate, or make less severe, agriculture's impact and to adapt to the effects of changing climates. As environmental activist Meredith Niles argues, "We must undertake both the enormous task of reducing our carbon emissions now to avert the worst, while at the same time adapting our society to the vast and multitudinous effects of unavoidable global climate change. Failing to do either will . . . have dire effects on a large portion of our world's population."[1] According to the Intergovernmental Panel on Climate Change (IPCC), there are significant opportunities for both adaptation and mitigation in the agricultural sector—in crop and grazing land management, water conservation, and livestock and manure management.

Improving Cropland Management

Croplands offer some of the best opportunities for adaptation and for mitigating harmful farm emissions. Because soil is the second largest pool of carbon on the planet (exceeded only by the ocean), the IPCC says that the agricultural option with the most mitigation (and adaptation) potential is soil carbon sequestration—increasing the amount of carbon that is stored in agricultural soils. As the 2007 IPCC report puts it, "Improved agronomic [crop-growing] practices that increase yields and generate higher inputs of carbon residue can lead to increased soil carbon storage."[2] Jeff Schahczenski and Holly Hill, specialists with the National Center for Appropriate Technology, a project funded by the U.S. Department of Agriculture, provide some detail about this option:

> The ability of agriculture lands to store or sequester carbon depends on several factors, including climate, soil type, type of crop or vegetation cover and management practices. The amount of carbon stored in soil organic matter is influenced by the addition of carbon from dead plant material and carbon losses from respiration, the decomposition process and both natural and human disturbance of the soil. By employing farming practices that involve minimal disturbance of the soil and encourage carbon sequestration, farmers may be able to slow or even reverse the loss of carbon from their fields.[3]

Carbon sequestration practices suggested by the IPCC include choosing crop strains that have increased tolerance to climate stresses such as high temperatures, drought, flooding, pests, diseases, and high salt content in soil. In addition, the IPCC recommends using more perennial crops, which keep more carbon underground than crops that are planted annually, and avoiding the practice of leaving fields fallow, or unplanted, since planted fields absorb much more carbon than unplanted ones.

Because soil is the second largest pool of carbon on the planet ... the IPCC says that the agricultural option with the most mitigation (and adaptation) potential is soil carbon sequestration—increasing the amount of carbon that is stored in agricultural soils.

Another increasingly popular method of carbon sequestration is called tillage management or direct seeding, which is basically defined as planting and fertilizing crops with reduced or zero tillage (plowing) of the soil. As the IPCC explains:

> Advances in weed control methods and farm machinery now allow many crops to be grown with minimal tillage (reduced tillage) or without tillage (no-till). These practices are now increasingly used throughout the world. Since soil disturbance tends to stimulate soil carbon losses through enhanced decomposition and erosion, reduced- or no-till agriculture often results in soil carbon gain.[4]

And because these low- and no-till practices mean that farm equipment is operated less frequently, less fossil fuel energy is used by farmers, thus cutting CO_2 emissions even further.

At the same time, low tillage strategies increase soil organic matter, strengthening soils and helping croplands adapt to climate changes. As the United Nations Food and Agriculture Organization (FAO) explains:

> Climate change adaptation for agricultural cropping systems requires a higher resilience against both excess of water (due to high intensity rainfall) and lack of water (due to extended drought periods). A key element to respond to both problems is soil organic matter, which improves and stabilizes the soil structure so that the soils can absorb higher amounts of water without causing surface run off, which could result in soil erosion and, further downstream, in flooding. Soil organic matter also improves the water absorption capacity of the soil during extended drought. FAO promotes low tillage and maintenance of permanent soil cover that can increase soil organic matter and reduce impacts from flooding, erosion, drought, heavy rain and winds.[5]

The 2007 IPCC report also suggests that emissions can be lowered by reducing reliance on synthetic fertilizers, manures, and pesticides, which are often applied excessively in conventional agriculture and not completely used by crops. One good

The Role of Genetic Engineering

Developing new plant varieties that can resist heat, drought, pests, weeds, and other climate impacts will be essential for agriculture to adapt to climate change. It is uncertain whether these new cultivars will be produced by traditional plant breeding methods—which involves breeding multiple generations of similar plants until undesirable traits are eliminated or desirable traits are enhanced, potentially using wild plants that have adaptive traits. Many scientists champion the use of genetic engineering (GE)—the science of altering the traits of plants by changing the genetic information encoded within their DNA—as a better method of plant development. The advantages of GE, supporters argue, are that it allows a precise gene transfer of a desirable gene into the new plant, it can transfer genes across species barriers, and it can achieve results faster.

GE faces both technological and ethical challenges, however. Many scientists as well as lay people oppose genetic crop manipulation because of the dangers that these synthetic varieties could pollute traditional crop strains that farmers have relied upon for centuries, possibly leading to less genetic diversity. Also, genetically altered species are typically developed and controlled by large corporations that are motivated largely by profits and that embrace expensive, industrial farming practices rather than low-tech, more sustainable agriculture. For example, many opponents to GE can be found in developing regions such as Africa, where multinational biotech corporations have urged local farmers to use GE crops that are heavily dependent on large amounts of expensive agrochemicals. These GE crops, sometimes called Frankencrops, are often patented, preventing farmers from saving seeds for future harvests and requiring them to buy new seeds every year. The real solution to climate change, GE opponents argue, is not GE crops but a return to more sustainable farming, which nurtures the soil and promotes biodiversity.

way of reducing fertilizer use, the IPCC says, is by planting legumes such as clover between the harvesting of one crop and the planting of the next. Legumes have the ability to fix nitrogen in the soil, which provides a natural fertilizer and allows farmers to avoid heavy use of synthetic nitrogen fertilizers that are responsible for a significant portion of nitrous oxide emissions. Another emissions-reducing farm practice is planting a temporary vegetative cover between crop plantings or between rows of crops so that excess nitrogen fertilizer in the soils will be used up. In addition, farmers can adjust the amounts and timing of fertilizer and pesticide crop applications based on more precise estimates of crop needs, or farmers can use slow-release fertilizers (which retard the microbial processes that lead to nitrous oxide formation). Pesticide use can be reduced by using natural plant-based pesticides or biological pest controls. Biological pest controls use organisms such as beneficial insects or parasites (ladybugs or mites, for example) to destroy plant pests.

Many of the IPCC's mitigation suggestions are similar to organic farming practices, which various studies have found to be effective at improving soils, sequestering carbon, and reducing emissions. A 2009 report by the FAO concluded that "there is scientific evidence that organic agriculture can sequester more carbon than conventional agricultural practices."[6] The FAO also has found that organic farms release fewer nitrous oxide emissions than conventional farms. At the same time, the FAO says, organic practices enrich soils and enable crops to better adjust to the effects of climate change. Organic farmers reject synthetic fertilizers and pesticides used by industrial agriculture and instead use organic manure fertilizers and biological pest controls. They also tend to seek crop diversity, often by growing a variety of crops as well as raising livestock, rather than growing just one or two crops year after year, as conventional farmers tend to do. In addition, organic farmers often employ crop rotation, legume cover crops, and similar strategies to build up soils, and they try to avoid polluting the air, soil, or water.

Drip irrigation, such as this system used in a South American winery, can save water and help plants survive droughts. Daniel Garcia/AFP/Getty Images.

Water Conservation

Because water is such a critical input for agriculture, improvements in water efficiency and conservation are also an important part of adaption and mitigation in the crop production sector of agriculture. According to the IPCC, about 18 percent of the world's croplands currently rely on irrigation rather than just rainfall, so improving existing irrigation systems and expanding irrigation to arid areas (where water supplies allow) could enhance carbon storage in soils and also help plants withstand hotter temperatures and other climate change effects. Similarly, use of more efficient irrigation technologies, such as drip irrigation and fertilization systems that direct water and fertilizer more precisely to plants, could reduce water usage, sustain plants during droughts, and also reduce the amount of nitrogen that is applied to plants, thereby reducing nitrous oxide emissions.

Responding to changing rainfall patterns could also provide important adaptation and mitigation benefits. Farm practices such as mulching and zero tillage, for example, could help retain moisture in soils during dry periods and also mitigate soil erosion in regions of intense rainfall. Harvesting and storing excess rainfall will also become more important in many regions where rainfall is expected to decrease, so water management of river basins, aquifers, and other freshwater areas will be forced to become more effective. Some policy makers in California, for example, have argued that the state needs to build more reservoirs to collect and store what is expected to be an ever-decreasing amount of rainfall and snowpack in future years.

Land Management and Grazing Decisions

According to the IPCC's 2007 report, agricultural emissions from croplands can also be reduced through land management decisions. Allowing or encouraging cropland to revert back to native vegetation, either completely or in specific areas such as the margins between fields, can increase carbon storage. Similarly, converting cropland to grassland for livestock grazing can improve carbon sequestration because grasslands typically are left untilled; this can also decrease nitrous oxide emissions because grasslands are not fertilized as much as croplands. Converting croplands back to wetlands achieves the same positive emission

AGRICULTURAL MITIGATION MEASURES AND THEIR EXPECTED IMPACT ON EMISSIONS

Measure	Examples	Mitigative Effects		
		Carbon Dioxide (CO$_2$)	Methane (CH$_4$)	Nitrous Oxide (N$_2$O)
Cropland management	• Agronomy	+		+/–
	• Nutrient management	+		+
	• Tillage/residue management	+		+/–
	• Water management (irrigation, drainage)	+/–		+
	• Rice management	+/–	+	+/–
	• Agro-forestry	+		+/–
	• Set-aside, land use change	+	+	+
Grazing land management/ pasture improvement	• Grazing intensity	+/–	+/–	+/–
	• Increased productivity (e.g., fertilization)	+		+/–
	• Nutrient management	+		+/–
	• Fire management	+	+	+/–
	• Species introduction (including legumes)	+		+/–
Management of organic soils	• Avoid drainage of wetlands	+	–	+/–
Restoration of degraded lands	• Erosion control, organic amendments, nutrient amendments	+		+/–
Livestock management	• Improved feeding practices		+	+
	• Specific agents and dietary additives		+	
	• Longer term structural and management changes and animal breeding		+	+
Manure/biosolid management	• Improved storage and handling		+	+/–
	• Anaerobic digestion		+	+/–
	• More efficient use as nutrient source	+		+
Bio-energy	• Energy crops, solid, liquid, biogas, residues	+	+/–	+/–

+ denotes reduced emissions or enhanced removal (positive mitigative effect); – denotes increased emissions or suppressed removal (negative mitigative effect); +/– denotes uncertain or variable response.

Source: Intergovernmental Panel on Climage Change, *Climate Change 2007: Mitigation of Climate Change: Contribution of Working Group III to the Fourth Assessment Report of the Intergovernmental Panel on Climate Change*, edited by B. Metz, O.R. Davidson, P.R. Bosch, R. Dave, and L.A. Meyer, New York: Cambridge University Press, 2007, p. 507.

results. These options could be viable, the IPCC says, for croplands that are no longer needed or that have become unproductive.

On lands that are already established as grassland grazing areas, other actions can be taken to lower emissions and help these lands survive climate impacts. For example, the IPCC suggests that avoiding overgrazing can optimize carbon levels in soils because the intensity and timing of grazing can affect plant growth, and overgrazing can cause plant death and soil erosion. Also, as with croplands, grazing lands can have their carbon sequestration ability increased through crop management practices such as improved plant and fertilizer choices, the planting of nitrogen-fixing legumes, and increasing irrigation. Studies have shown, for example, that introducing grass species that have deeper roots can both stabilize more carbon and resist drought. A project in California, called the Marin Carbon Project, has emphasized the importance of grassland management actions. As sustainability activist and author Warren Karlenzig writes, the project found that:

> The ability of grassland soil to sequester carbon is . . . directly related to how grasslands and rangelands are maintained. When trees and shrubs are left in grassland areas, for instance, there is 30% extra carbon sequestration. Adding compost or manure also greatly increases soil carbon sequestration. . . . Tilling soil, on the other hand, has a negative impact on carbon sequestration.[7]

Also, better fire control on grasslands prevents the combustion of organic matter that produces emissions.

Changes in Livestock Management

After land management, livestock management—mostly concerning ruminants such as cattle and goats—is the area that offers the most potential for adaptation and mitigation. Curbing livestock methane emissions may be critical because of rapid global population growth and the rising demand for meat products. The FAO has projected that by 2050, livestock numbers worldwide will double, approximately doubling livestock-related greenhouse gas emissions.

The 2007 IPCC report focuses on three categories of methane reduction in livestock production: improved feeding practices, dietary additives, and management and breeding changes. Studies have shown, for example, that methane emissions from livestock can be reduced by feeding animals more concentrated feed rather than allowing them to forage on grasses. Other changes in feeding such as adding certain oils or oilseeds to the animals' diet, improving the quality of pastures, and increasing the protein content of feed can also help reduce emissions while making animals healthier and better able to face climate stresses. In addition, the IPCC notes that there are numerous substances that can be added to animals' diets to suppress methane production. These include certain antibiotics, compounds made of elements such as iodine and bromine, plant materials and essential oils, and probiotics such as yeast. Researchers are also working to develop a vaccine against methane-producing bacteria, and certain hormonal additives can lessen lifetime emissions by improving animal growth. More long-term ideas for methane reduction involve ways of increasing production through breeding changes and better management. If meat-producing animals can be encouraged to grow faster, for example, they reach slaughter weight more quickly, producing fewer lifetime emissions per animal. And breeding changes—to develop animals that produce less methane or that are more resistant to heat or other climate impacts—could be helpful for both adaptation and mitigation purposes. Breeding changes can be accomplished either by traditional selective breeding techniques or through genetic engineering practices, which are more controversial.

Another major focus for reducing greenhouse gas emissions related to livestock production is manure management. The IPCC notes that methane emissions of most animals worldwide are negligible because they are raised in open fields, where the manure dries and decomposes in an oxygen environment. But when manure decomposes anaerobically (without oxygen), such as when it is stored in lagoons or tanks by large-scale concentrated animal facilities, methane emissions are far higher. The 2007 IPCC report, therefore, addresses this source, suggesting that methane can be reduced in these storage facilities by cooling, using solid covers, separating solids from slurry, or by capturing the methane emitted and using it as an energy source—an option that could also produce another profit source for animal producers.

A 2009 study by the Worldwatch Institute made similar suggestions for reducing emissions from livestock, but also proposed broader ideas, including better regulating large animal producers and supporting small family farms that are more environmentally sustainable. Of course, another way of reducing livestock emissions is by limiting the amount of meat in human diets. As animal activist Noam Mohr wrote in a report for the environmental group EarthSave, "the best way to reduce global warming in our lifetimes is to reduce or eliminate our consumption of animal products. Simply by going vegetarian, we can eliminate one of the major sources of emissions of methane."[8]

Bioenergy

Some climate experts suggest that growing more crops for producing bioenergy—renewable energy made available from materials derived from biological sources—is another effective agricultural mitigation option, because this bioenergy would displace emissions-producing fossil fuels. Various types of biomass could be used for this purpose, including grains such as corn (which is the largest source of U.S. biofuel), sugarcane, switchgrass (a tall grass native to North America), and even crop residues such as the husks and stalks left over after corn is harvested. These crop materials are either burned directly or processed into liquid fuels such as ethanol or diesel fuel that produces fewer CO_2 emissions than regular gasoline.

The IPCC, however, explains in its 2007 report that "The net benefit to atmospheric CO_2 . . . depends on energy used in growing and processing the bioenergy feedstock."[9] This is the main criticism of biofuel crops—that they often require substantial amounts of fossil fuel, producing minimal net emissions savings. In addition, the use of agricultural land for growing biofuel crops means less land for growing food, which could cause food shortages or increased food prices—a scenario that food experts say occurred in recent years when many U.S. corn crops were diverted from food to biofuel purposes. The IPCC, therefore, concludes that it is not yet clear whether the world can effectively exploit the potential for bioenergy in a way that will produce significant mitigation benefits. Thus, many experts suggest that other options for agricultural emissions mitigation and adaptation may provide more dependable ways of navigating future climate change, at least in the near future.

Notes

1. Meredith Niles, "Organic Farming Beats Genetically Engineered Corn as Response to Rising Global Temperatures," *Grist*, January 16, 2009. www.grist.org.
2. Intergovernmental Panel on Climate Change (IPCC), "Chapter 8: Agriculture," in *Climate Change 2007: Mitigation: Contribution of Working Group III to the Fourth Assessment Report*, edited by B. Metz, O.R. Davidson, P.R. Bosch, R. Dave, and L.A. Meyer, Cambridge, UK: Cambridge University Press, 2007, p. 506. www.ipcc.ch.
3. Jeff Schahczenski and Holly Hill, "Agriculture, Climate Change and Carbon Sequestration," National Sustainable Agriculture Information Service, 2009. http://attra.ncat.org
4. IPCC, "Chapter 8: Agriculture," p. 507.
5. Food and Agriculture Organization of the United Nations, *Adaptation to Climate Change in Agriculture, Forestry, and Fisheries: Perspective, Framework and Priorities*, Rome: Author, 2007, pp. 10–11. www.fao.org.
6. Maria Müller-Lindenlauf, "Organic Agriculture and Carbon Sequestration: Possibilities and Constraints for the Consideration of Organic Agriculture Within Carbon Accounting Systems," Food and Agriculture Organization of the United Nations, December 2009, p. 21. www.fao.org.
7. Warren Karlenzig, "Massive Rangeland Carbon Sequestration Opportunities May Hinge on Urban Compost," *World Changing*, December 4, 2009. www.worldchanging.com.

8. Noam Mohr, "A New Global Warming Strategy: How Environmentalists Are Overlooking Vegetarianism as the Most Effective Tool Against Climate Change in Our Lifetimes," Earth Save International, August 2005. www.earthsave.org.
9. IPCC, "Chapter 8: Agriculture," p. 511.

CHAPTER 9

Conclusion: The Future of Farming

The challenges ahead for agriculture in a warming world are daunting. Essentially, farmers will be asked to engineer a second Green Revolution to meet demand for a growing world population while also reducing their emissions and adapting to difficult climate changes. Scientists say that this feat will require farmlands to become much more productive, but in many areas of the world, farmers may struggle just to maintain reasonable crop yields in the face of hotter and drier conditions, extreme weather events, and other climate impacts. In addition, many farmers must work with an environment that is already degraded and polluted from years of unsustainable farming and water use practices. And this new revolution must extend to regions that the first Green Revolution never reached—places such as Africa, where many people are very poor and struggle to survive on small plots of farmland.

Developing Climate Policies

Developing the right international and national policies on climate change will be of vital importance to the future of farming, agricultural and climate experts say. On the international level, combating and adapting to climate change involves getting nations around the world to work together on the issue. So far, most of the work has been focused on mitigation. The United Nations, through the Kyoto Protocol—a 1997 international treaty that seeks to reduce greenhouse gas emissions—has had some success in encouraging the adoption of national climate policies in some countries and in creating a global carbon market that allows for the international trading of carbon credits in order to reduce emissions. This carbon trading system—often called cap and trade—works by setting a limit on each country's emissions, and then allowing countries with high emissions to buy credits from countries that have low emissions, so that overall global emissions are reduced.

Yet the international goal of slowing emissions on a global scale has proved elusive. The Kyoto treaty covered only industrialized countries and set relatively modest limits on carbon emissions. And Kyoto never regulated the world's two biggest emitters—China, which was outside the scope of the treaty as a developing country, and the United States, which never agreed to abide by the treaty—so it failed to reduce overall global greenhouse gas emissions. According to scientists, global emissions from fossil fuel use have increased substantially since 1997. Moreover, the Kyoto treaty expires in 2012, and the effort to develop a replacement treaty so far has failed. At the international climate summit held in December 2009 in Copenhagen, Denmark, negotiators could not agree on binding national carbon caps—the key to reining in global emissions and creating a booming worldwide carbon trading market.

Ultimately, however, it is the governments of each individual country that bear the responsibility of preparing for and responding to climate changes that will affect their citizens and businesses. As the United Nations International Panel on Climate Change (IPCC) notes in its 2007 report, "a wide variety of national policies and instruments are available to governments to create the incentives for mitigation action."[1] National governments, for example, can adopt legislation and regulations to limit carbon emissions and encourage adaptations by implementing carbon taxes, tradable carbon permits, agricultural research and development programs, agricultural subsidies, and various other financial incentives. In terms of agriculture and the food supply, governments can set farm and food standards, modify trade policies, negotiate voluntary agreements with agricultural corporations, and take various other actions to ensure that domestic agriculture companies take the necessary actions to reduce emissions and prepare for coming climate changes. The nations of the European Union adopted an Emissions Trading System in 2005, but the power of many national governments to act on climate change has been restricted by political and economic considerations. In the United States, for example, big-farm lobbyists have tried their best to derail passage of climate legislation, both in the House of Representatives, where the American Clean Energy and Security Act (H.R. 2454) passed in June 2009, and in the Senate, which had not considered a climate bill as of late 2010.

'Hunger will be one of the major impacts of climate change. It may be the defining human tragedy of this century.'

In addition, most countries are only beginning to consider and implement climate change adaptation measures. In the United States, the federal-level National Oceanic and Atmospheric Administration's Regional Integrated Sciences and Assessments (RISA) program has been assigned the job of researching adaptation issues, and some state and local governments are developing and implementing climate change adaptation plans. There is still a lack of specific information about exactly how climate change will affect local areas, however. Also, this issue is one of many competing for resources during times of economic stress, so even in developed countries, officials struggle to make it a priority.

Aid for Poor Countries

Developing nations face even more obstacles in addressing climate change. Governments in these countries typically lack the resources and technical knowledge required to implement effective actions to reduce emissions and adapt their agricultural sectors to climate change. The task is made even harder for these countries because most of their farmers are poor, small-scale farmers, many of whom already face challenges such as deteriorated soils, environmental pollution, and insufficient water resources. Climate researchers say that the billions of small farmers in these developing regions will be hardest hit by future climate changes, so providing them with climate solutions and assistance will be critical.

A 2009 report by the international relief and development organization Oxfam, for example, studied the effects of today's climate changes on small farmers in Asia, Africa, and Latin America and found that global warming is already causing major changes in seasons. Such shifts are threatening people's ability to farm and feed themselves. Oxfam concludes that various kinds of aid are needed—everything from reliable weather forecasts and food storage facilities to water management tools and greater access to new crop varieties that are drought-tolerant and fast-maturing. According to the group, this aid to developing countries will cost at least $150 billion a year. Otherwise, Oxfam warns,

> Hunger will be one of the major impacts of climate change. It may be the defining human tragedy of this century. Millions of people in countries that already have food security problems will have to give up traditional crops and agricultural methods as they experience changes in the seasons that they and their ancestors have depended upon. The social upheavals that result—such as migration and conflict—may mean that this change in the functioning of our planet affects more people than any other.[2]

Sustainable Agriculture
Another big challenge for agriculture will involve deciding on the best methods of mitigation and adaptation to climate change.

Although modern, large-scale industrial agriculture has been highly productive, experts agree it has resulted in widespread water pollution and degraded soils. The environmental think tank World Resources Institute, for example, estimates that nearly 40 percent of the world's agricultural soils are depleted. So there is a growing awareness that farming must become more sustainable to save the natural environment and ensure that farmlands remain productive for the future. A sustainable agriculture model may also help farmers with mitigation and adaptation to climate change. The IPCC's recommendations for mitigating emissions, for example, focus on such options as crop management, water conservation, and improved manure management—sustainable practices that the IPCC says would both cut emissions and benefit the environment.

Some agriculture activists and experts, however, argue for a complete transformation of the global farming system and an end to government policies and trade agreements that support industrial farming. For example, the International Assessment of Agricultural Knowledge, Science and Technology for Development (IAASTD), a project initiated by the World Bank in partnership with the United Nations Food and Agriculture Organization (FAO) and others, released a report in 2008 that concluded that a fundamental change in farming practices is needed to prevent soaring food prices, world hunger, climate change, and environmental disasters. The report rejected genetically engineered and biofuel crops and the entire chemical-laden, energy-intensive industrial farming model, arguing that small-scale farms and more ecological and sustainable farming methods are the key to agriculture's future. IAASTD's director, scientist Robert Watson, has called for a new agricultural revolution, explaining,

> Agriculture has a footprint on all of the big environmental issues, so as the world considers climate change, biodiversity, land degradation, water quality, [etc., it] must also consider [agriculture, which] lies at the centre of these issues and poses

some uncomfortable challenges that need to be faced. We've got to make sure the footprint of agriculture on climate change is lessened, we have to make sure that we don't degrade our soil, we don't degrade the water, we don't have adverse effects on biodiversity. There are some major challenges, but we believe that by combining local and traditional knowledge with formal knowledge these challenges can be met."[3]

The growing influence of organic and sustainable farming methods could soon translate into concrete policies that can be applied by countries and agricultural corporations to reduce environmental damage and improve agricultural soils and products. In recent years, for example, the FAO has launched an initiative to encourage various developing countries to adopt "good agricultural practices"—guidelines for implementation at farm level that seek to promote sustainable production, safe and healthy food handling, high standards of animal welfare, and jobs with fair incomes. Even large industrial farm operations may benefit in the future from making some adjustments toward greater sustainability. Sustainable farming advocate Fred Kirschenmann, for example, has argued that industrial agriculture is highly dependent on both stable climate conditions and cheap oil, but neither will exist in the future, so it will be imperative for farms to become more resilient, diverse, and sustainable in order to survive. As Kirschenmann points out, "Sustainability is about the future—about keeping something going, maintaining something into the future."[4]

Not everyone supports this drive toward more sustainable agriculture, however. Supporters of genetically engineered crops, for example, claim that the new crop varieties cannot be bred fast enough by conventional methods, so genetically created crops are needed to adapt to climate changes such as heat, drought, and flooding. And many agricultural experts argue that it will be impossible to increase yields and production without using industrial, large-scale agriculture methods. Other experts see a middle course. University of Minnesota researcher Jonathan Foley, for example, has argued, "We need a third way to solve the crisis. Let's take ideas from both sides, creating new, hybrid solutions that boost production, conserve resources and build a more sustainable and scalable agriculture."[5]

Some Positive Signs

This debate about the future direction of agriculture will likely continue for years, and the outcome remains uncertain, but if the world's farmers are able to launch a second Green Revolution, it is likely to be very different from the first. Farmers face far more complex problems today. The solutions of the past no longer seem to work, and new ingenuity appears to be required.

Many commentators say high-tech advances will lead the way in helping farmers to both mitigate emissions and adapt to future climate changes. One rapidly developing technology called "precision agriculture," some agricultural experts suggest, will revolutionize farming in coming years. Precision agriculture involves the use of satellites and Global Positioning System (GPS) monitors to send data to sophisticated farm machinery about the condition of farmland—factors such as where the soil is moist or eroded and where crops are thriving or struggling. This information then allows farmers to precisely apply the appropriate amounts of seed, water, fertilizer, and pesticides so that maximum efficiency in food production is realized. This technology could prevent much of the over-fertilization that is creating nitrous oxide emissions, and it could also be an effective adaptation tool.

Other advances in crop breeding—using biochemistry, genetics, or traditional methods—could lead to more productive and nutritious crops. Plants that have more effective root systems, that require less fertilizer, that grow in untilled soil, and that can withstand warmer and drier conditions could allow crop yields to remain high despite climate changes and could also lessen agriculture's impact on the environment. Other plants that once contained little nutrition could be bred to become super-plants, full of vitamins and minerals needed by the hungry poor. Researchers are also experimenting with other new technologies, including growing food in deserts by using nearby abundant saltwater that has been desalinated through a low-energy process; using microbes to reduce plants' needs for fertilizers and pesticides; and using robots to monitor and harvest crops.

Another ray of hope comes from recent predictions about population growth, which have noted that the rate of growth is slowing because of declining fertility in many countries. Population experts suggest therefore that the world population may stabilize somewhere far below the 9 billion previously projected by 2050, and it could possibly decrease afterward. With a less rapidly expanding global population, farmers will have a much better chance of feeding the world.

The future, therefore, is full of both challenge and promise for agriculture. On the one hand, the future of farming will be largely a time of crisis during which farmers will need to fight climate change, limit farm emissions, and try to preserve soils and water supplies. At the same time, the coming crisis may create opportunities for new farm technologies and innovations in farm practices that could make agriculture both more productive and more environmentally sustainable over the long term.

Notes

1. International Panel on Climate Change, "Chapter 8: Agriculture," in *Climate Change 2007: Mitigation: Contribution of Working Group III to the Fourth Assessment Report*, edited by B. Metz, O.R. Davidson, P.R. Bosch, R. Dave, and L.A. Meyer, Cambridge, UK: Cambridge University Press, 2007, p. 19. www.ipcc.ch.
2. Oxfam, "Suffering the Silence: Climate Change, People, and Poverty," July 6, 2009. www.oxfam.org.uk.
3. International Assessment of Agricultural Knowledge, Science and Technology, "Inter-Governmental Report Aims to Set New Agenda for Global Food Production," (news release), March 31, 2008. www.agassessment.org.
4. Frederick L. Kirschenmann, "Frederick L. Kirschenmann's Remarks upon Accepting the Glynwood Medal for Distinguished Leadership in Sustainable Agriculture" (speech), New York City, October 27, 2008. www.glynwood.org.
5. Quoted in *New York Times*, "Can Biotech Food Cure World Hunger?" October 26, 2009. http://roomfordebate.blogs.nytimes.com.

Glossary

adaptation Actions taken to adapt, or adjust, to climate changes brought by global warming.

agricultural gross domestic product An economic measure of a nation's total agricultural output.

animal production The raising of domestic animals for the production of meat, eggs, and dairy products.

arable land Terrain that is suitable for agricultural cultivation.

atmosphere The gaseous envelope surrounding the earth.

bioenergy/biofuel A fuel produced from biomass, such as agricultural crops and wastes, grasses, and trees. Examples include ethanol and biodiesel.

biomass Organic matter either living or dead, such as trees and plants, as well as municipal solid waste.

cap and trade A system that sets an overall limit on the amount of allowable greenhouse gas emissions and allows countries or companies that cannot meet emission reduction targets to buy carbon credits from other countries or companies that are exceeding emission reduction goals.

carbon caps A limit on the amount of carbon dioxide that a country or company is permitted to release into the atmosphere.

carbon dioxide (CO_2) A gas formed during respiration, combustion, or organic decomposition; one of the greenhouse gases that contributes to global warming.

carbon fertilization Improvements in crop growth and production caused by rising CO_2 concentrations that are part of global warming.

carbon sequestration The process of capturing carbon dioxide before it enters the atmosphere and permanently storing it underground or under the ocean waters.

cheatgrass (*Bromus tectorum*) An invasive winter annual grass, unpalatable to livestock, that originated in Europe and Asia and came to the United States in the 1890s.

climate change Long-term global weather changes caused by global warming.

corn belt A region located in the U.S. Midwest, where farmers grow large quantities of corn.

crop yield The amount of agricultural output that crops produce each season.

deforestation The conversion of forested land into roads, agricultural land, or some other kind of non-forested land.

El Niño Southern Oscillation (ENSO) A climate pattern in the tropical Pacific Ocean that involves warming or cooling of surface waters that can cause droughts, floods, and other weather disturbances on land areas around the world.

emissions The release of greenhouse gases into the atmosphere through the burning of fossil fuels and various other sources, which causes global warming.

emissions trading A market mechanism that allows emitters (countries, companies, or facilities) to buy emissions from or sell emissions to other emitters; also called carbon trading.

ethanol An alternative automobile fuel produced from corn or other biomass materials.

extreme weather Weather events—such as unusually strong rainstorms or snowstorms, high winds, intense heat or cold waves, more frequent cyclones or hurricanes, or long droughts—caused by global warming.

fisheries Areas where fish are caught or produced, including both wild fishing areas and fish farms, or aquaculture.

food accessibility Having the resources and ability to obtain available food supplies.

food availability The process of producing and distributing crops and other foods.

food security Having access to a sufficient amount of safe and nutritious food. According to the Food and Agriculture Organization of the United Nations, food security has four components—food availability, food accessibility, food utilization, and food system stability.

food system stability The ability of global and local food processing, storage, and marketing systems to operate efficiently to package and transport food safely and efficiently to areas of need.

food utilization Having available and accessible food that provides in a safe and reliable way the nutrients needed by people.

fossil fuel A hydrocarbon deposit, such as petroleum, coal, or natural gas, created in underground deposits millions of years ago from the decomposition of plants and animals.

genetic engineering (GE) The science of altering the traits of plants or animals by changing the genetic information encoded within their DNA.

glacier A year-round mass of ice that is located on, and moves over, land.

global warming An increase in the average temperature of the earth's atmosphere and ocean that can cause climate changes.

grasslands Grazing lands typically found in areas of low rainfall, such as the North American prairies, but also in regions with higher precipitation levels, such as parts of Europe and New Zealand, as well as parts of North and South America.

Green Revolution A term referring to dramatic increases in crop production beginning in the 1960s in the United States and other developed nations as a result of the increased use of petroleum energy that was used to power farm equipment and of petrochemicals that were developed into cheap fertilizers and pesticides.

greenhouse gases (GHGs) Gaseous constituents of the atmosphere, both natural and human-produced, that trap energy from the sun and warm the earth. The Kyoto Protocol refers specifically to the following six GHGs: carbon dioxide, methane, nitrous oxide, hydrofluorocarbons, perfluorocarbons, and sulfur hexafluoride.

gross domestic product (GDP) An economic measurement of a nation's total economic output.

groundwater Water located underneath the ground, either in porous soil or in spaces in rock.

heat stress Stress on animals created by high temperatures, which can lead to declines in eating and grazing, decreases in dairy milk production, and altered conception rates; also called thermal stress.

industrial crops Crops grown for industrial purposes or products, such as oilseeds (plants grown for their oils—such as flax, sunflowers, and groundnuts including peanuts); gums and resins; food sweeteners; beverages (such as coffee and tea); fibers (grown to make paper, cloth, or rope); and medicinal and aromatic plants.

industrial farming/agriculture A form of modern farming that refers to the industrialized production of crops, livestock, poultry, or fish, typified by the heavy use of synthetic fertilizers on crops, an emphasis on monoculture crop production, and the production of animals in concentrated indoor or outdoor facilities; also called factory farming.

Intergovernmental Panel on Climate Change (IPCC) Established in 1988 by the World Meteorological Organization and the UN Environment Programme, the IPCC is a scientific body charged with providing the world a clear scientific view on the current state of climate change and its potential environmental and socioeconomic consequences.

Kyoto Protocol An international agreement adopted in December 1997 in Kyoto, Japan. The protocol sets binding emission targets for developed countries that would reduce their emissions to, on average, 5.2 percent below 1990 levels.

methane A flammable gas produced by decomposition of organic matter; one of the greenhouse gases that causes global warming.

mitigation Techniques or processes that reduce or offset the adverse impacts of climate change.

nitrous oxide (N_2O) A gas emitted naturally from soils (and from excess nitrogen added to soils) or as a by-product of combustion; one of the greenhouse gases that causes global warming.

no-till/low till farming A farm technique of avoiding plowing or disturbing soil and simply planting new crops amid the debris of previous crops.

organic farming/agriculture A type of agriculture that employs organic manure fertilizers and biological pest controls; seeks crop diversity (often mixing a variety of crops with livestock); uses crop rotations, legume cover crops, and similar strategies to build up soils; and seeks to avoid polluting the air, soil, or water.

rain-fed land Terrain that receives enough rainfall to grow crops.

rangelands Grazing lands in dry regions that include vegetation such as desert plants, scrub, and chaparral.

salinization The infusion of freshwater sources with salt or seawater as a result of sea-level rise, one of the projected impacts of global warming.

snowpack Naturally formed, packed snow. It is especially common in mountainous regions and often melts in springtime, providing a source of freshwater.

soil erosion The loss of topsoil due to increased water flows, high winds, or other climate impacts caused by global warming.

sustainable farming/agriculture A type of agriculture that seeks to avoid toxic inputs or outputs so that it can be sustained without long-term damage to the environment.

For Further Research

Books

Albert Bates, *The Biochar Solution: Carbon Farming and Climate Change*. Gabriola Island, BC, Canada: New Society, 2010.
Explains the use of biochar, a type of charcoal, as a soil supplement to help combat climate change.

Arvid Bjurstrom, *The Role of Agriculture in Carbon Capture and Climate Change*. Hauppauge, NY: Nova Science, 2010.
Highlights the effects that agriculture has on carbon capture and climate change.

John Boardman and David Favis-Mortlock, *Climate Change and Soil Erosion*. Hackensack, NJ: World Scientific, 2007.
Discusses the impact of climate change on agricultural soils.

Ariel Dinar, Rashid Hassan, Robert Mendelsohn, and James Benhin, *Climate Change and Agriculture in Africa: Impact Assessment and Adaptation Strategies*. London: Earthscan, 2008.
Provides an analysis of the potential economic impacts of climate change, and the value of adaptation measures, in Africa.

Andrew Kimbrell, *Fatal Harvest: The Tragedy of Industrial Agriculture*. Sausalito, CA: Foundation for Deep Ecology, 2002.
Criticizes the corporate, industrial model of agriculture as a destroyer of the environment.

Rattan Lal, M. Suleimenov, B.A. Stewart, D.O. Hansen, and P. Doraiswamy, eds., *Climate Change and Terrestrial Carbon Sequestration in Central Asia*. New York: Taylor & Francis, 2007.
Summarizes current knowledge of terrestrial carbon sequestration in Asia, including such topics as water resources, soil degradation, soil management, and sustainable agriculture.

Rattan Lal, Norman Uphoff, Bobby A. Stewart, and David O. Hansen, *Climate Change and Global Food Security*. Boca Raton, FL: CRC Press, 2005.

Argues that there is an impending agricultural crisis due to rising food demand and the future impacts of climate change on yields and food production.

Anna Lappe and Bill McKibben, *Diet for a Hot Planet: The Climate Crisis at the End of Your Fork and What You Can Do About It*. New York: Bloomsbury USA, 2010.
Addresses the major role industrial agriculture plays in today's climate crisis, explains the value of organic farming, and argues for using wise eating habits to combat climate change.

Eric Lichtfouse, *Climate Change, Intercropping, Pest Control and Beneficial Microorganisms*. New York: Springer, 2009.
A collection of articles discussing various environmentally sustainable farm practices and techniques.

———, *Genetic Engineering, Biofertilisation, Soil Quality and Organic Farming*. New York: Springer, 2010.
A collection of articles analyzing problems with modern agricultural practices and proposing sustainable solutions.

———, *Organic Farming, Pest Control and Remediation of Soil Pollutants*. New York: Springer, 2009.
A collection of articles on the value of organic farming and the need for sustainable pest and soil management.

David Lobell and Marshall Burke, eds., *Climate Change and Food Security: Adapting Agriculture to a Warmer World*. New York: Springer, 2009.
Explores the different methodologies and data that scientists use to understand climate's effects on food security, and explains the ways that crops and farmers can respond.

Cynthia Rosenzweig and Daniel Hillel, *Climate Variability and the Global Harvest: Impacts of El Niño and Other Oscillations on Agro-Ecosystems*. New York: Oxford University Press, 2008.
Describes the current efforts to study and predict the El Niño–La Niña cycle and develop a global climate risk management system.

Shyam S. Yadav, David L. McNeil, Robert Redden, and Sharanagouda A. Patil, *Climate Change and Management of Cool Season Grain Legume Crops*. New York: Springer, 2010.

Addresses the issues of legume production management technologies, plant ecological response, nutrient management, biological nitrogen fixation, molecular approaches, potential cultivars, and biodiversity management under climate change.

Periodicals and Internet Sources

Agriculture Business Week, "Developing Cool Rice for a Warmer World," February 7, 2009. www.agribusinessweek.com.

John M. Antle, "Climate Change and Agriculture: Economic Impacts," *Choices*, First Quarter 2008. www.choicesmagazine .org.

Sharon Begley, "China and India Will Pay," *Newsweek*, August 26, 2009. www.newsweek.com.

David Biello, "Farmed Out: How Will Climate Change Impact World Food Supplies?" *Scientific American*, September 30, 2009. www.scientificamerican.com.

Darius Dixon, "Experts Warn Climate Change Is Beginning to Disrupt Agriculture," *Climatewire*, June 17, 2010. Reprinted at www.scientificamerican.com.

Shelby Lin Erdman, "Study: Global Warming Sparked by Ancient Farming Methods," CNN.com, August 18, 2009. www.cnn.com.

Jared Flesher, "New Way to Farm Boosts Climate, Too," *Christian Science Monitor*, March 12, 2009. www.csmonitor.com.

Laurie Goering, "Climate Change Is Worsening Food Insecurity, Experts Say," *Alternet*, November 2, 2009. www.alertnet.org.

Mae-Wan Ho, "GM-Free Organic Agriculture to Feed the World," *Institute of Science in Society*, April 18, 2008. www .i-sis.org.uk.

Verlyn Klinkenborg, "Why I Still Oppose Genetically Modified Crops," *Environment 360*, September 17, 2009. http://e360 .yale.edu.

Gowri Koneswaran and Danielle Nierenberg, "Global Farm Animal Production and Global Warming: Impacting and Mitigating Climate Change," *Environmental Health Perspectives*, vol. 116, May 2008, pp. 578–82. www.ncbi .nlm.nih.gov.

Timothy J. LaSalle, "How to Stop Global Warming and Hunger at the Same Time," Treehugger.com, June 19, 2008. www .treehugger.com.

Judy Lowe, "How Will Climate Change Affect Agriculture?" *Christian Science Monitor*, September 30, 2009. www .csmonitor.com.

Daniel Martin, "'Eat Fewer Sausages to Save the Planet from Global Warming,' Britons Warned," *Mail Online*, November 26, 2009. www.dailymail.co.uk.

Mongabay.com, "Secretary of Energy Warns of Dire Future for Agriculture in California," February 5, 2009. http://news .mongabay.com.

Newsweek, "Coping with Climate," December 30, 2008. www .newsweek.com.

———, "So Shall You Reap," September 24, 2009. www .newsweek.com.

Meredith Niles, "Organic Farming Beats Genetically Engineered Corn as Response to Rising Global Temperatures," *Grist*, January 16, 2009. www.grist.org.

Melinda Peer, "Planting the Seeds for Sustainability," *Forbes .com*, September 25, 2009. www.forbes.com.

Elisabeth Rosenthal, "Environmental Cost of Shipping Groceries Around the World," *New York Times*, April 26, 2008. www.nytimes.com.

Hilary Rosner, "The Future of Farming: Eight Solutions for a Hungry World," PopSci.com, August 7, 2009. www.popsci .com.

Ariel Schwartz, "Kangaroo Farming Could Reduce Global Warming," CleanTechnica.com, August 11, 2008. http://cleantechnica.com.

Mark Steil, "New Farming Practices in Middle of Global Warming Debate," *MPR News*, December 9, 2009. http://minnesota.publicradio.org.

Jim Tankersley, "California Farms, Vineyards in Peril from Warming, U.S. Energy Secretary Warns," *Los Angeles Times*, February 4, 2009. www.latimes.com.

E.G. Vallianatos, "Energy Farming Worsens Global Warming," *Seattle Post-Intelligencer*, September 19, 2007. www.seattlepi.com.

Bryan Walsh, "Climate Change Catch-Up," *Time*, June 1, 2008. www.time.com.

Web sites

Climate and Farming (www.climateandfarming.org). Resource materials to help farmers make practical and profitable responses to climate change.

Climate Change and Agriculture in Africa (www.ceepa.co.za). A Web site devoted to providing information on the activities of a World Bank project called Climate, Water and Agriculture: Impacts and Adaptation of Agro-ecological Systems in Africa.

Consultative Group on International Agriculture Research— CGIAR and Climate Change (www.cgiar.org). Information from an international, nongovernmental science organization on the effects of climate change upon the rural poor in developing countries.

Environmental Defense Fund—Global Warming (www.edf.org). An environmental group's positions on climate change.

Intergovernmental Panel on Climate Change (IPCC) (www
.ipcc.ch). A scientific body set up by the United Nations
Environment Programme to provide objective information
and reports about climate change science.

International Food Policy Research Institute (www.ifpri.org).
An international agricultural research organization's analyses of policies for meeting the food needs of the developing
world.

Natural Resources Defense Council (www.nrdc.org). This environmental organization's Web site contains a special section
on global warming and related issues.

Pew Center on Global Climate Change (www.pewclimate.org).
A nonpartisan, science-based organization that provides
both basic and in-depth information about all aspects of the
climate change issue.

The Sierra Club (www.sierraclub.org/globalwarming). The
Sierra Club is a grassroots environmental organization ac-
tive on global warming issues.

Union of Concerned Scientists (www.ucsusa.org). This science-
based organization provides in-depth information and news
about global warming and is a proponent of sustainable
agriculture.

U.S. Department of Agriculture, Economic Research Service
(www.ers.usda.gov/Briefing/GlobalClimate). Features
"Global Climate Change," a federal government briefing on
the impacts of climate change on U.S. agriculture and agriculture's contribution to climate change.

U.S. Environmental Protection Agency—Climate Change (www
.epa.gov/climatechange). An informative federal government Web site on the science, effects, and solutions to
climate change.

U.S. Global Change Research Program (www.globalchange
.gov). An initiative that coordinates and integrates federal
research on changes in the global environment and their
implications for society.

World Resources Institute (www.wri.org). An environmental
think tank's views on climate change.

Worldwatch Institute (www.worldwatch.org). Information on
and analysis of climate change, the food supply, and sustainable agriculture from an independent research organization.

Index

About the Author

Debra A. Miller is a writer and lawyer with a passion for current events, history, and public policy. She began her law career in Washington, D.C., where she worked on legislative, policy, and legal matters in government, public interest, and private law firm positions. She lives with her husband in Encinitas, California. She has written and edited numerous books, anthologies, and other publications on historical, political, health, environmental, and other topics.